Coding In Delphi

Nick Hodges

Coding In Delphi

Nick Hodges

This book is for sale at http://leanpub.com/codingindelphi

This version was published on 2014-02-21

ISBN 978-1-941266-03-8

Tweet This Book!

Please help Nick Hodges by spreading the word about this book on Twitter!

The suggested tweet for this book is:

I just bought "Coding in Delphi" by Nick Hodges. Give it a look! #codingindelphi

The suggested hashtag for this book is #codingindelphi.

Find out what other people are saying about the book by clicking on this link to search for this hashtag on Twitter:

https://twitter.com/search?q=#codingindelphi

Contents

Foreword

I first met Nick during a Delphi 1 pre-launch "boot-camp" that was held at the brand new Borland campus in Scotts Valley, California. We had invited a cadre of developers, authors and long-term luminaries to get some in-depth training and presentations directly from the development team and product management. Enthusiastic and exuberant are adjectives that don't fully characterize my first impressions of him. He was never afraid of asking questions and absorbed the information quickly.

I cannot talk about Nick without also discussing TSmiley. Inquisitive and curious, Nick embraced Delphi without reservation. To that end, Nick wasn't satisfied with what Delphi did, but was just as keen on learning about how it did it. To that end, Nick holds the honor of producing one of, if not the first non-Borland built component. In order to learn about Delphi component building, he built TSmiley. In this one simple component all the core aspects of using Delphi's Pascal language to extend and enhance the VCL framework were demonstrated. You see, Delphi component building is all about the code.

I had the pleasure of working closely with Nick during his time at Borland and then Embarcadero. Nick held the position of Product Manager for a while then managed a portion of the Delphi R&D team. Nick was never afraid to challenge assumptions and actively stand up for the Delphi developer community. Even though Nick's position didn't require him to write code, he didn't let that stop him. He was always looking for ways to keep his programming skills as sharp as possible. As new features were developed, Nick was always right there to give them a workout. To this day there is a large amount of code written by Nick that remains a key portion of the overall regression and unit-testing process. Nick discovered that some of the best ways to learn about new code is to test that new code. It is not without irony that this process requires code to be written.

It stands to reason that Nick would end up here; writing a book with a single focus on the code. That is the engine that drives all the other revolutionary features of Delphi. Without the code, there would be no "Visual" in the Visual Component Library (VCL). In fact, Delphi has always been about getting the developer to their code as quickly as possible. The VCL and the newer FireMonkey component frameworks make the use and construction of UI, database, connection and others as simple as possible. Its ultimate goal is to allow the developer to focus on their task, which is to produce an application that solves a specific problem. It is the code that is written in between those UI, database and connection components that make up the application.

Developers at all levels will be able to use the information contained within this book. It doesn't matter if you're relatively new to Delphi or programming or you've got many years of experience. If there is one common trait I've found among software developers, it is their desire to learn. Learning a new technique or figuring out how to apply that technique to one's unique situation is part of the excitement of being a software developer. This is right up there with the thrill experienced when some thought, idea or concept comes to life within the computer. When a developer sees their running application, rarely do they think about the few moments they spent arranging some controls on the User Interface. They feel a sense of pride about that one difficult and thorny problem they solved through the clever use of code. At the end of the day, to a developer, it is really all about the code.

Allen Bauer

Introduction

Over the years, I've spoken in front of a lot of Delphi developers. The one thing that I notice is that there are a lot more of you Delphi guys than the average Delphi guy thinks. There are Delphi folks everywhere. Also, I have noticed that a lot of Delphi developers are "behind". That is, they are either using an older version of Delphi, or they aren't using or aren't even aware of all the features in the newer versions of Delphi that they are using. Something I like to do when I'm in front of folks is ask a few questions about what people are doing. I'm always saddened that the response to questions like "Who is doing unit testing?" or "Who is taking advantage of Generics?" is pretty meager.

This is particularly true for the language features and the run-time library. It's quite easy to move forward with an older code base, utilizing the new features in the IDE and adding new things to your app using the new high level frameworks and components that come in the newer versions. For example, you might have been developing an application since Delphi 3, moving forward through various versions. Along the way, you may have added some DataSnap functionality, started using the Code Insight features in the IDE, and when you moved to XE2, you start poking around with FireMonkey.

But it's fairly easy to ignore the new language features that come along with those new versions. For instance, two powerful language features were added in Delphi 2009: generics and anonymous methods. Both are features that enable the development of really cool code and frameworks. But if you didn't understand or feel the need for them, then it was pretty easy to simply not use them. You can still do all kinds of great stuff in Delphi without them, but with them, well, you can write some really beautiful, testable, and amazing code.

For instance, a relatively new framework that exists only because of these new language features is the Spring Framework for Delphi, or Spring4D, as I'll refer to it in this book. Spring4D is a feature rich framework that provides a number of interesting services, including a wide variety of collections that leverage generics, an Inversion of Control container, encryption support, and much more. I view Spring4Dsolid as much a part of the Delphi RTL as SysUtils is. Using Spring4D in your code will make many, many things easier and cleaner. But many Delphi developers don't know this yet.

If the above is familiar, this book is for you: The Delphi developer that hasn't quite yet made the leap over into the cool and amazing things that you can do with the latest versions of the Delphi language. This book is all about introducing these new language features and some of the intriguing things you can do with them. It will take a look at these new language features, and then expand into some of the open source frameworks that have sprung up (no pun intended) as a result. It will then show you techniques that you can use to write SOLID[1], clean, testable code.

You won't find much of anything about the IDE or the higher level frameworks here. Screen shots will be few but code examples many. You won't find anything about how to build better user

---

[1]http://butunclebob.com/ArticleS.UncleBob.PrinciplesOfOod

interfaces or fancy components. What you will find are ways to make your code much cleaner, much more powerful, and way easier to maintain.

This book is all about the cool, new code you can write with Delphi. It won't matter whether you are building a VCL or an FM application. I've titled it "Coding in Delphi" because I want to make it a book that shows you simple examples of how to use powerful features – that, is about the *code*. These language features are indeed advanced features – they are new relative to, say, the case statement – and thus many of you are beginners to them. By the end of this book, you won't be.

The approach I'm taking for this book is to try to distill things down to the very basics. The examples will be very simple but the explanations deeper. I believe that if you can understand the basic idea in a simple example, it is but a small leap to using those ideas in more complex code. There is no point in giving complex examples when you can get the main thrust using fundamental implementations that illustrate advanced ideas. Between the code in this book and in the samples online (https://bitbucket.org/NickHodges/codingindelphi[2]) you can learn all the precepts and then begin applying them to your own code. In other words, nothing fancy here, just the basics – it is then up to you to use these ideas in your own code.

This book is not done – it's instead a living document. Since it is self-published on a platform that makes iteration very easy, I plan on having frequent releases to fix typos (which will, I'm sure, sneak through despite my best efforts), improve examples and descriptions, and keep up with technology changes. Owners of the PDF should get notifications of new versions automatically. If you are reading a paper version of this book, I'm sorry I can't deliver fixes to your hard-copy – perhaps some day that will be possible.

The book will be done when you guys say it is done. Maybe, it will never be done because Delphi keeps growing and expanding. I guess we'll see.

As a result, I'm totally open to feedback – please feel free to contact me at nickhodges@gmail.com with suggestions corrections, and improvements. Please join the Google Plus group for the book.[3] I may even add whole new chapters.

Thanks for your purchase – this book was a labor of love, so every sale is icing on the cake.

Nick Hodges

Gilbertsville, PA

---

[2]https://bitbucket.org/NickHodges/codingindelphi
[3]https://plus.google.com/communities/110978417023349293804

Acknowledgements

Writing a book like this is a lot of work. But it can't all be done by the author. I had a lot of help.

First I want to thank everyone in my Google Plus group that proofread the early drafts. I'm very grateful. I'd like to particularly thank the following people who really went above and beyond in their help.

These four gentlemen made great comments and suggestions in the Google Plus group.

- Stefan Glienke
- Kenneth Cochran
- Bruno Sonnino
- Andrea Raimondi

Bill Meyer read the first finished draft from cover to cover, finding countless typos and providing excellent feedback. I'm grateful.

I need to give a special level of thanks to Jeroen Pluimers who really went above and beyond in helping with this book. He read and re-read it numerous times. He contributed coding samples and managed much of the code repository for the book. I am very grateful to him for all of his superb help. I probably should have put his name on the cover.

I'd like to thank Allen Bauer for writing the Foreword and for answering some particularly sticky questions that only he can answer. Allen has been a good friend over the years and I'm grateful to know such a smart, nice guy.

Diane Moser proofread this book and made countless corrections and improvements. I'm grateful.

My daughter Piper designed the cover using an idea my wife had. I'm very proud of her design skills.

It almost goes without saying, but I'd like to thank my family. Writing a book is a lot of work, and they put up with me being distracted and on the computer more than I should have been. I'd particularly like to thank my daughter Timber who I think missed her Papa a lot.

And finally I'd like to thank my precious and beautiful wife Pamela. She encouraged me and supported me to write this book and it simply would not have happened without her. I love you.

Frameworks used in Coding in Delphi

This book is about writing code in Delphi. As a result, it uses a number of open source frameworks to facilitate the coding techniques that are discussed herein. I refer to them here at the beginning of the book to enable you to retrieve the code and get them set up before we begin.

All of the frameworks below are available via source control. I recommend that you pull or clone the source code in accordance with the instructions in the source repository. This way you can very easily keep up with the latest changes and fixes. If you have questions about how to setup and use Subversion, Git, or Mercurial, please see Appendix A.

Delphi Spring Framework

The Delphi Spring Framework is a large collection of libraries, including data structure collections, a dependency injection container, encryption, and other features. In this book we'll be closely examining the collections and dependency injection features.

Homepage: http://www.spring4d.org/[4]

Source Location: https://bitbucket.org/sglienke/spring4d[5]

Repository Type: Git

License: Apache License V2.0[6]

DUnitX

DUnitX is an xUnit testing framework for Delphi 2010 and greater. It uses attributes to define tests and test fixtures.

Source Location: https://github.com/VSoftTechnologies/DUnitX[7]

Repository Type: Git

License: Apache License V2.0[8]

---

[4]http://www.spring4d.org/
[5]https://bitbucket.org/sglienke/spring4d
[6]http://www.apache.org/licenses/LICENSE-2.0
[7]https://github.com/VSoftTechnologies/DUnitX
[8]http://www.apache.org/licenses/LICENSE-2.0

Delphi Mocks

Delphi Mocks is a complete isolation framework for Delphi XE2 and up. It enables the creation of stubs and mocks for use in unit testing frameworks.

Source Location: https://github.com/VSoftTechnologies/Delphi-Mocks[9]

Repository Type: Git

License: Apache License V2.0[10]

DSharp

DSharp is a multi-featured set of libraries for Delphi, including mocking (for Delphi 2010 and up), data-binding, a Dependency Injection container, an MVVM framework, Aspect oriented programming, and more.

Source Location: https://bitbucket.org/sglienke/dsharp[11]

Repository Type: Subversion

License: New BSD License[12]

---

[9]https://github.com/VSoftTechnologies/Delphi-Mocks
[10]http://www.apache.org/licenses/LICENSE-2.0
[11]https://bitbucket.org/sglienke/dsharp
[12]http://opensource.org/licenses/BSD-3-Clause

1 Exceptions and Exception Handling

1.1 Introduction

Added into Delphi back at the very beginning with Delphi 1, exception handling was a fundamental change to the way we thought about and wrote our code. Unfortunately, despite almost twenty years of use, there are still many misconceptions and misunderstandings about how exceptions work and especially about how they should be used.

In this chapter, I'll look at how exception handling should be done. I'll start out with examples of the wrong way to use and handle exceptions. Using that as a base, I'll then discuss proper ways for using exception handling. Used improperly, exception handling can actually cause more problems and errors than it prevents. Used correctly, they can aid you in writing clean, well-designed code that is easy to maintain. I'll assume that you are familiar with exception handling syntax, and the basics of how exceptions work.

1.2 Structured Exception Handling

An exception is a language feature that allows a programmer to stop execution of a process or thread immediately, but intercept that "stop" at any point in the call stack when necessary. Structured exception handling is a combination of language features and good design that makes use of exceptions in order to allow programmers to make useful assumptions when writing code and, most critically, respond correctly when those assumptions turn out not to be true.

These assumptions are often called preconditions – they are things which must be true for a method to succeed. For example, a method that deletes a record from a database might have the precondition that the user is logged into the database before it is run. Because the program's user interface is structured to only run the method after logging in, a programmer might assume that this precondition will always be true. But what happens when the database server crashes?

The programmer could address this by checking to ensure that the server is connected at the start of every method. But this is by no means the only precondition, and may lead to duplication of code. Or the programmer might forget to include all of the relevant checks when writing a new method.

Structured exception handling provides an elegant solution to all of these issues. It ensures that a method will fail if the preconditions are not fulfilled, and furthermore that it fails in such a way that the developer can recognize and respond to the failure.

1.3 How Not to Use Exceptions

Much of the work I do involves working on existing projects that have been struggling – most often because of poor design – and rewriting code that wasn't well done in the first place. One of the most common coding errors I see is the misuse of exceptions – sometimes really ugly misuse. To start off, I'll go through a few "Don'ts" for exception handling use, discussing why each is not a good technique.

Don't Eat Exceptions

Probably the most common — and really egregious – misuse of exceptions is the "eating" of exceptions. Very often I'll see code like this;

```
try
  SomeRoutineThatSometimesCausesAHardToFindAccessViolation
except
end;
```

For the Love of Baby Elvis, please do not do this. As you can see, this code will "eat" **any** exception that gets raised in the called routine. Very often, the code in the try block raises an error that isn't easily found, and rather than do the hard work of actually tracking down the error, the programmer will take the easy way out and just eat the exception. Sometimes, the reason for eating the exception is nothing more than the desire to never let the end user see any error messages. If that is your goal, however, you should do so in such a way that you don't conceal the errors from the rest of your code, as well.

Rest assured, the user will see no error messages as a result of this code. Every single exception that could possibly arise from this code will be suppressed – database exceptions, out of memory exceptions, hardware failures, anything. This means that your program may return incorrect results while appearing to succeed. It is better to clearly indicate failure than to silently make an error that could result in an incorrect paycheck or worse!

The only time I can think of when simply eating an exception is acceptable is when you need to prevent an exception from propagating across module boundaries. If you are doing inter-module programming, for instance, code that will run in a DLL, you shouldn't let any exceptions escape from the current module. In this case, using an empty exception handler on the outer boundary of a DLL can do that for you. But unless such is the case, eating exception handlers like this should be considered a gross error and a coding horror. Even in this situation, you should somehow log the exception, or acknowledge it in some way. Eating exceptions means that the information about the error – which could make fixing it easy – is gone for good. Your customer may never realize there is a problem, and even if they do you may not be able to figure out why it happened and how to fix it. Bottom line: just don't eat exceptions.

Don't Generically Trap Exceptions

Sometimes I see code that looks like this:

```
try
  SomeCodeThatMightCauseAProblem
except
  on E: Exception do
  begin
    MessageDlg(E.Message, mtWarning, [mbOK], 0);
  end;
end;
```

And I think "That's sort of like drinking Caffeine-Free Diet Coke" – in other words, why bother? This code doesn't do anything other than report an exception that will likely be reported anyway. Actually, it does one other thing, and that is to stop the exception in its tracks. The exception will be handled locally, and will never be allowed to escape the current scope, In addition, it will trap all exceptions, including ones that you may very well not want trapped.

The only time that you might even consider using this construct – which is only slightly better than eating the exception altogether – is when you know that the calling routine doesn't want to handle any exceptions or when the calling routine expects to handle the specific exception. For instance, the TClientDataset has an OnReconcileError event that actually passes an exception into it. If you were doing some batch processing with a Clientdataset, then allowing this exception to bubble up the stack will stop the loop. In this case, you might want to generically trap all the exceptions that are passed into the event handler.

Don't Go Looking For Exceptions

Exceptions are fairly expensive in terms of processing power to create and handle, and so you shouldn't be creating them as a matter of course. In addition, you shouldn't be creating them on purpose or using them for the purpose of error checking, per se.

For instance, you might be tempting to do something like this admittedly contrived example:

```
function StringIsInteger(aStr: string): Boolean;
var
  Temp: integer;
begin
  Result := True;
  try
    Temp := StrToInt(aStr);
  except
    Result := False;
  end;
end;
```

This code will do what you want it to do – determine whether a string holds a valid integer, but it will also probably raise a lot of exceptions that can hurt performance, especially if the number of times that it is expected to return false is high.

Performance issues aside, this is an incorrect use of exception handling because it is not a violation of a precondition for the method. The method is clearly designed to accept non-integer arguments, hence it should not use the exception method, even internally, to handle such a case. A better implementation of this method would use the `TryStrToInt` function in `SysUtils`.

Don't Use the Exception Handling System as a Generic Signaling System

```
type
  TNormalBehaviorException = class(Exception);

...

begin
  SomeCodeThatDoesNormalThingsAndDoesntHaveAnyErrors;
  raise TNormalBehaviorException.Create('Something perfectly normal' +
                                        'and expected happened');
end;
```

You might be tempted to write the above code as a means of signaling the calling code about some type of information, especially if your custom exception handler has additional information in it that can be 'signaled' back to the calling routine. Remember that exceptions are a flow control mechanism as well as a tool for conveying information. Raising exceptions when you simply want to send a message can have unexpected consequences for program flow.

Raising unneeded exceptions can be very irritating, even if your application always captures and handles the exception in question, or your custom exception descends from EAbort and won't result in an error message that they user will see. For one thing, this is a pretty processor-intense way of signaling and passing information. Secondly, the error will appear at design-time, driving you and other developers crazy, as well as at run-time, annoying users. (A very popular third-party library does this sort of thing, and it drives me to distraction.) As a general rule, if you are raising an exception that pretty much requires your users to add that exception to the list of exceptions to be ignored by the IDE, then you should think twice about raising that exception at all.

1.4 How to Use Exceptions Properly

Now that you've seen some of the ways not to use exceptions, here are some tips for properly using Delphi's exception handling system.

Use Exceptions to Allow Your Code to Flow Without the Interruption of Error Handling Code

One of the main purposes of exception handling is to allow you to remove error-checking code altogether and to separate error handling code from the main logic of your application. With exception handling, you can write your code as if nothing ever goes wrong, and then wrap that code up with try...except blocks to deal with any of the errors and problems that may occur. This enables your code to run more efficiently, as it isn't constantly checking parameters and other data to make sure that it is in the proper form before doing anything with it.

One way to separate code and exceptions is to handle exceptions centrally. TApplication has an event that allows you to do just that – the OnException event. You can use this event to deal with all exceptions of any type that aren't otherwise handled by your application. You can use this event to log your exceptions, or provide specific handling for specific types of exceptions.

Application Writers Should Trap Exceptions

As will be discussed below, components and library code should be the main source of exceptions; that is, components and library code should be the place where most exceptions are created and raised. When writing applications, there is little need for you to create and raise exceptions. Application writers should mainly be about the business of handling exceptions that are raised by components and library code.

Trap only specific exceptions

As noted above, you should never eat exceptions. What you should do instead is to trap only specific exceptions that might reasonably be expected to occur in your code. If you are doing a lot of math, you might want to trap for EMathError exceptions. If you are doing a lot of conversions, you might want to trap for EConvertError. Likewise, when doing database work, you might want to look out for EDatabaseError exceptions.

But even those errors might be a bit general. For instance, within database code, there may be specific descendant classes of EDatabaseError that occur when specific database actions are taken. So if you are opening a query, perhaps you should trap for exceptions that occur only on the opening of datasets, rather than the more generic EDatabaseError.

As I mentioned above, I see code that eats exceptions added because the developer (or manager, or someone not thinking very clearly) never wants the user to see any errors. The way to deal with that is to trap the specific exception that the user is seeing. For instance:

```
try
  SomeCodeThatRaisesAnEConvertError;
except
  on E: EConvertError do
  begin
  // Deal with this specific exception here
  end;
end;
```

This code is better than simply eating all exceptions, no matter what you do with the exception, because at the very least, it will only trap that one exception and not every exception that comes along.

Furthermore, database exceptions (and some others, like COM errors) generally include an error code, and you may wish to trap only errors with a certain error code and allow others to surface. You can do this as follows:

```
try
 SomeCodeThatRaisesAnEConvertError;
except
  on E: EIBError do
  begin
   if E.ErrorCode = iSomeCodeIWantToCatch then
   begin
     // Deal with this specific exception here
   end else
   begin
     raise; // re-raise the exception if it's not the one I handle
   end;
  end;
end;
```

Another reason to trap exceptions as far down the hierarchy chain as possible is that there may be future exceptions created that descend from the more generic Exception class. For instance, if you have this code:

```
try
  SomeDataset.Open
except
  on E: EDatabaseError do
  begin
  // Handle exception
  end;
end;
```

And then I come along and declare:

```
type
  ENxStrangeDatabaseError = class(EDatabaseError)
```

My new and strange exception will be trapped by your code, and perhaps that isn't what you want to have happen. Obviously you can't prevent this from ever happening, as a developer can descend from any existing exception, but you can make it happen less by trapping exceptions at the bottom of the class diagram.

Bottom line: Trap exceptions as far down the class hierarchy as you can and only trap those exceptions that you are planning on handling.

Component Writers and Library Code Writers Raise Exceptions

Exceptions do not mysteriously appear. The vast majority of them are created and raised within framework code. (Some can actually occur outside the purview of Delphi code.) And it is perfectly acceptable for you to raise your own exceptions as well.

As a general rule, you should raise specific exceptions in your library code and in your components. That way, application writers can trap those specific exceptions in their code as discussed above.

You should write library code and component methods in such a way that they do one of two things: they either execute successfully and return, or they raise an exception. Application writers should assume the same thing – that a routine that is called will either return successfully (with a valid result if the routine is a function) or that it will raise an exception.

Raise Your Own Custom Exceptions

When you do raise exceptions, always raise your own custom exceptions. For instance, I have a library of code that I use in a file called NixUtils.pas. In that file I declare

```
NixUtilsException = class(Exception);
```

And any exceptions that I raise in the routines found there are either of that type or are descendants of `NixUtilsException`.

Doing this allows users of your library code and components to do what I've exhorted you to do above: trap only specific exceptions. Don't be afraid to declare your own exception classes and then descend from them, even to the point of having specific exceptions for specific routines. This allows your users to trap exceptions with whatever level of granularity they require.

Let Your Users See Exception Messages

If you are tempted to hide all errors from the tender eyes of your users, ask yourself this question: Which is worse, having your users see error messages, or having the application roll along as if nothing has gone wrong, possibly leaving a trail of bad calculations and corrupt data?

Sadly, I've seen a lot of code that answers that question with the latter option rather than the former. That's how you end up with code that has empty exception handlers and eats any and all exceptions.

Exceptions occur because something is wrong. Ignoring them can have unexpected results. Eating an `EOutOfMemory` exception can have disastrous results, because your application – and your users – will continue on as if nothing bad has happened, when in fact bad things have happened.

Users are fearful of dialog boxes, as many user interface experts have noted, but if your dialog box actually gives them something to do, then the dialog boxes may be more useful than they normally are.

Feel Free To Provide Good Exception Messages

You don't have to be terse and uninformative with your errors. When you raise an exception, feel free to make the message passed up the stack as informative as you like:

No need to do this:

```
type
  ESomeException = class(Exception);

procedure CauseAnException;
begin
  raise ESomeException.Create('Boring message');
end;
```

when you can do something like this:

```
type
  ESomeException = class(Exception);

procedure CauseAnException;
begin
  raise ESomeException.Create('An exception occurred, and here is exactly what ha\
ppened....');
end;
```

Write full, descriptive error messages. You can even include the procedure name, the TObject.ClassName, or whatever you like in the message.

You can, in fact, enhance an existing exception's error message, set the new exception as the "outer" exception, and raise your new exception with the original exception as the inner exception:

```
type
  EMyException = class(Exception);
  EMyInnerException = class(Exception);

procedure RaiseInnerException;
begin
  try
    raise EMyException.Create('This is the message from EMyException');
  except
    on E: EMyException do
    begin
      E.RaiseOuterException(EMyInnerException.Create('This is the message from FM\
yInnerException'));
    end;
  end;
end;
```

Since the exception handler includes the call to raise an outer exception, the exception isn't being eaten here, but the code provides information about where the error occurred, etc. You include information about where users can go for help, what they should do if the error persists, etc.

Provide Two Versions Of A Library Routine

Sometimes people don't like routines that return exceptions. Well, okay, why not accommodate them? The RTL does this – it sometimes provides two functions that do the same thing, with one raising an exception on failure and the other returning nil or some error value, depending on the result. The FindClass/GetClass pair comes to mind. FindClass locates and returns a class type by name, and if it can't find it, it raises an exception. GetClass, on the other hand, will simply return nil if the class cannot be found.

1.5 Conclusion

It's quite easy to fall into the trap of using exception handling improperly. The ability to make errors and problems 'disappear' is quite tempting. However, misunderstanding and misusing exceptions in your code can lead to some real problems, including untraceable crashes and data loss. The proper use of exceptions can make your code easier to read an maintain. Use exceptions wisely, and you'll be able to product robust, clean code.

2 Using Interfaces

2.1 Introduction

Just about everything that I write about in this book will be predicated on the use of interfaces. If you aren't using interfaces for just about everything you do, you need to start. I once tweeted

"If I could teach a new programmer one thing it would be this: Program to an interface, not an implementation.[1]"

Program to an interface, not an implementation

When you use interfaces, you can decouple yourself from any particular implementation. When one module of code isn't directly connected to another module of code, that code is said to be "loosely coupled". And as I will probably repeat countless times throughout this book, loosely coupled code is a very good thing.

2.2 Decoupling

All through this book, I'll talk a lot about decoupling your code and why that is really good. But a definition here is probably a good idea. Code can be said to be decoupled when your classes are designed in such a way that they don't depend on the concrete implementations of other classes. Two classes are loosely coupled when they know as little about each other as possible, the dependencies between them are as thin as possible, and the communication lines between them are as simple as possible.

In other words, decoupling is the process of limiting your dependencies to abstractions as much as possible. If you want to write good, clean code, you will try to couple only to abstractions; interfaces are abstractions. Much of what will be discussed in this book will be about using interfaces to code against abstractions. As I tweeted above, this is critical to writing good code that is easy to maintain.

In Delphi, decoupling starts by limiting what goes into the uses clause of any given unit. Every time you use code from another unit, you are creating a connection or a coupling of code. You should try as much as possible to expose units that declare only Delphi interfaces to other units. You should

---

[1]https://twitter.com/NickHodges/statuses/122114771318345728?tw_i=122114771318345728&tw_e=permalink&tw_p=archive

endeavor to put as little as possible in the `interface` section of your units. This will allow you to limit the coupling of your code – if you don't put it in the interface section, it can't be coupled to.

Once you have limited the connections between your units, you can then start limiting the connections between your classes. Classes have to connect to each other somehow – otherwise you can't build a system. But if you are going to connect things together, you want those connections to be as thin as possible. That's where interfaces come in.

Of course to program against an interface, you have to first know what an interface is.

2.3 What are Interfaces?

Interfaces are kind of hard to describe, but I'll have to try anyway, eh?

The dictionary describes an interface as:

> Interface – n. : A point where two systems, subjects, organizations, etc., meet and interact.

In the general case of code, an interface is the means by which code modules – usually classes – interact with each other to perform specified actions. Your code needs to do something, and interfaces are the definitions that allow code modules to work together.

That's the general definition – but Delphi has a reserved word `interface` which has a specific syntactical meaning and which provides a specific functionality. So what are interfaces in Delphi?

Interfaces are an abstract definition of functionality.

Okay, that sounds all intellectual, doesn't it, but it's true.

An interface declaration defines a set of properties and methods that you can use for a specific purpose. Interfaces declare and require no specific implementation for that purpose. They define what a class can do and limit the exposure of a class to only those things defined by the interface.

Of course, an interface must be implemented to be useful. And when you use an interface, you ultimately don't care about **how** it is implemented; you just know that you can call the methods and properties on the interface and the functionality you need will be provided. Implementation hiding (i.e., abstraction) is one of the main purposes of using interfaces.

2.4 Interfaces Everywhere

We see interfaces in our lives every day. Electric plugs are an interface. In the United States, our electric plugs have two vertical, rectangular slots for the phase and neutral nodes, and one round hole below for the grounding node. What is that but a definition of functionality? In order to implement the interface, you merely provide a plug that matches the interface, and your device will work.

A plug is just an interface

You can plug in hair dryers and computer monitors – the interface doesn't care. These items could be said to be "powerable" as a result.

Delphi developers are already doing this with interfaces, perhaps without even realizing it. Well, a form of interfaces, anyway. Every Delphi unit has a section in it called the interface section, right? This section declares the functionality that the unit provides. Only those things declared in the interface section of a unit may be used by other units. Classes and methods in the interface section are implemented in the implementation section of the unit, and that implementation is hidden from users of the unit. You can't put implementing code in the interface section. Code declared in a unit's implementation section is not usable outside the unit. In this way, a unit is a simple example of what interfaces are for: declaring functionality and hiding (but still providing) an implementation.

The second main reason for using interfaces is the one discussed above – decoupling. If you program against interfaces, you can write your code in such a way that it is never coupled – or "connected" – to anything but that interface. The more loosely coupled your code is, the less likely it is that a change in one place will affect code in another. In addition, by coding against an interface, you can replace the implementation with a better one without breaking anything. (Once again, I'll be harping on loosely coupled code throughout the book, and particularly in the discussion about Dependency Injection.) For now, the point is that interfaces are critical in decoupling your code, and that decoupled code is good.

The code for an interface is actually quite simple: It is a declaration of methods and properties without an implementation. However, that simplicity can make them hard to understand. Interfaces as a language feature were first introduced in Delphi 3, and I remember very clearly thinking "Huh? Why in the world would you want to use interfaces?" Little did I know then, however, that interfaces are probably the single most effective coding tool in your arsenal. Once you truly understand what interfaces are for and what they can do, it will make it so much easier to write clean, uncoupled, testable code. (We'll be talking about the meaning of "testable code" in the chapter on Unit Testing.)

Interfaces are similar to abstract classes in that they can define a set of methods that must be implemented. They differ in that they have no implementation themselves, whereas an abstract class might have implementation of non-abstract methods. The most analogous thing to an interface would be an abstract class that has all abstract methods and thus no implementation at all.

Abstract Classes	Interfaces
...can contain abstract methods which are normally overridden by descendants	...contain a list of methods that must be implemented by the implementing classes
...can be but normally are not instantiated	...can't be instantiated because they are merely a definition of functionality
...can contain concrete functionality which will thus be provided to all descendants	...have no functionality at all attached to them. They depend entirely on their implementing class for functionality.
...are not reference counted and must be manually freed.	...are normally reference counted and their implementing instance will by default be freed automatically.
...can only have single-inheritance descendants	...can be combined together in an implementing class that implements multiple interfaces

Interfaces cannot themselves be instantiated, and are only useful when implemented. They are pure references. An interface is implemented by a class that declares in its type definition that it will implement a given interface. The implementing class must then provide an implementation for the exact set of methods and properties as declared in the interface. A failure to do so will result in a compiler error. Any class can implement any interface – that is one of the strengths of the feature.

A class may also implement any number of interfaces. In this way, Delphi can provide a functionality similar to multiple inheritance without all the trappings and difficulties of that feature. (I don't know if he originated the statement, but Zack Urlocker, Delphi's original Product Manager, has been quoted as saying "Multiple inheritance is the GOTO of the nineties." I always loved that, even though the nineties were a while ago.) Interfaces can also inherit from, and thus enhance, another single interface.

2.5 A Simple Example

For example, here is a declaration of a very simple interface:

```
type
  IName = interface
  ['{671FDA43-BD31-417C-9F9D-83BA5156D5AD}']
    function FirstName: string;
    function LastName: string;
  end;
```

Interfaces consist of a name (in this case, IName) and a declaration of methods and properties. By convention, Delphi interfaces start with the letter "I," but that is not enforced. You can create interfaces with any name you want, but using the "I" makes it easier to identify an interface in your code. An interface includes no "real" code for implementing functionality. An interface cannot declare fields, variables or constants. Nor can they define scope such as private, protected, etc. It is purely a declaration of capability. Thus, every member of an interface is essentially public.

In the case above, the interface says "Hey, when I am implemented, I'll give you information about someone's name." It tells you what functionality is available. It does not tell you how the functionality will be implemented. In fact, the interface doesn't care, and the user of the interface shouldn't care either. The implementation of the interface might do any number of things to get the name information – randomly pick from a list, grab it from a file, or pull it from a database or some other data store. The interface itself doesn't care and cannot dictate where the name comes from. All the interface knows is that it's implementer will return a string – that's it. It's not even guaranteed that the string will be a person's name, though that is obviously the intent.

 Note that the declaration of the interface has a Globally Unique Identifier (GUID) right after the initial declaration. This GUID is used by the compiler to identify this interface. You can use an interface without the GUID, but much of the RTL and most frameworks that take advantage of interfaces will require a GUID be present. (You can generate a GUID any time you want in the IDE by typing CTRL+SHIFT+G)

Of course, the purpose here is to create an implementing class that has some meaning when it goes into "Get me a person's name" mode. For instance, you might have a form that gathers the name from the user. You might be iterating over records in a database and use the interface to grab each name as they are iterated. The point is that it doesn't matter what the implementing objects are or what they do – they just produce a name when treated as an IName interface.

2.6 Implementing an Interface

But of course, as you've guessed, an interface can't do anything without an implementing class. Fortunately, Delphi makes it really easy to implement interfaces. To do so, you need to declare a class as implementing an interface, and then make sure that class implements all the methods in the interface.

In order to implement IName, you might declare a class as follows:

```
type
TPerson = class(TInterfacedObject, IName)
protected
    function FirstName: string;
    function LastName: string;
  end;


function TPerson.FirstName: string;
begin
  // Could get this from a database or anywhere, but for demo purposes,
  // we'll hard-code it
  Result := 'Fred';
end;


function TPerson.LastName: string;
begin
  // Could get this from a database or anywhere, but for demo purposes,
  // we'll hard-code it
  Result := 'Flintstone';
end;
```

Here are some things to note:

- The class declares IName after the base class. (The base class is TInterfacedObject – we'll discuss this special class below.) It declares and implements the two functions required by IName.
- The declaration of the two methods is defined as protected. The interface doesn't care what the visibility is – it will allow access to any implementing method regardless of the visibility – but by declaring the methods as a visibility not available to users of the class, you can ensure that the only way to talk to the class is via the interface.

Interfaces can also declare properties. In order to do so, the interface must declare explicit getters and setters. They are both necessary because interfaces cannot declare field variables.

```
type
  IAged = interface
  ['{3D7E1BBE-6273-47A9-9CB7-CB31FDF6AB69}']
    function GetAge: integer;
    procedure SetAge(aValue: integer);
    property Age: integer read GetAge write SetAge;
  end;
```

 Note that this means that the getters and setters can be called directly from the interface - even if they are private in the implementing classes. Of course, you should leave those getters and setters totally alone and only access them via the property.

Thus, you can declare an implementing object like so:

```
TAgedThing = class(TInterfacedObject, IAged)
private
  FAge: integer;
  function GetAge: integer;
  procedure SetAge(aValue: integer);
public
  property Age: integer read GetAge write SetAge;
end;
```

A class can implement any number of interfaces, so you can have a class declaration like so:

```
TAgedPerson = class(TInterfacedObject, IName, IAged)
private
  FAge: integer;
  function GetAge: integer;
  procedure SetAge(aValue: integer);
public
  function FirstName: string;
  function LastName: string;
  property Age: integer read GetAge write SetAge;
end;
```

wherein the TAgedPerson class provides an implementation for all the interfaces included in its declaration.

2.7 Some Further Things to Note:

- An implementing class can have any number of other fields and methods that it needs or requires, as long as it has the methods defined by the interface. If you fail to provide all the necessary methods, the compiler will give you an error until you do. But the class can be as complex as you need it to be (though generally you should frown on complex classes, right?)
- The base class can be any base class as long as it implements the necessary methods for Delphi's interface reference counting. (TInterfacedObject does this automatically for you – more on TInterfacedObject and what reference counting is will be discussed below.) But I want to stress again – the base class can be anything. It could be a class you created. It could be a VCL class. It could be TButton or TClientDataset or anything. It doesn't matter, and the interface doesn't care, as long as you provide implementations for all the necessary methods.

2.8 Interface Inheritance

Interfaces can inherit from other interfaces, so you can declare an interface like so:

```
IFullName = interface(IName)
['{07E8CFE2-4C2B-41F4-8934-D9D3B5BE39BC}']
  function FullName: string;
end;
```

In this way, the child interface will require an implementation for all its declared methods as well as those of its parent. Any class that implements IFullName will have to provide implementations for all of the methods in IFullName as well as IName.

Note that an implementation of the child interface is not an explicit implementation of the parent. An implementation must explicitly declare the interface that it wants to implement, even if it declares all the required members. That is, unless a class explicitly lists a given interface as part of its declaration, it cannot be used to implement that interface. Thus, you need to list both parent and child interfaces in an implementing declaration if you want use it as both the parent and child interface.

Actually, the use of the phrase 'interface inheritance' is a bit misleading – it's not really true inheritance in that you can't override a method from a parent interface, and there is no polymorphic behavior that results. 'Interface augmentation' might be a better way to phrase it.

2.9 Other Things to Think About

Here are a few things to think about when creating and dealing with interfaces:

- As a general rule, you should declare interfaces in their own unit, preferably one interface per unit. Interfaces should be defined separately from any implementation or any other code. It's very tempting to declare an interface and a class that implements it in the same unit, but you should resist this temptation. Keep interfaces separate and completely decoupled from any particular implementation.

- It's a good idea to have interfaces be specific and to the point. If you have a large interface – one with many methods, you might consider breaking it down. This is known as the Interface Segregation Principle (http://en.wikipedia.org/wiki/Interface_segregation_principle) – the idea that interfaces shouldn't have methods that the implementer doesn't need. There are times when it's okay to have a larger interface, but don't be afraid to have interfaces with just a handful of – or even one – methods, and don't be shy about having a class implement more than one interface.

- Interfaces can be used as abstractions for your code, but not all interfaces are necessarily abstractions. If you have a "leaky" abstraction, then your interface isn't truly an abstraction. A leaky abstraction is one that allows implementation details to sneak through, thus dictating a certain kind of implementation. Say you had an interface called IDataSource and that interface had a method called GetConnectionString. Having that method appears to strongly imply the notion of a database that requires a connection string. An implementation of IDataSource might use a collection or a list, and so the notion of a connection string shouldn't be part of the implementation. In this case, the implementation detail of having a connection string has "leaked through" your attempt at abstracting the notion of a data source. Along those lines, if your interfaces are merely a reproduction of the public class you use to implement it, then it is very likely that you have a leaky abstraction. In this case, you should go back to the drawing board and refactor your code accordingly.

2.10 About TInterfacedObject

Okay, so there's a bit more to it than what I've discussed so far. In Delphi, interface references are reference counted. That is, the compiler keeps track of each reference to the implementing object, increasing the count when a reference is added and decreasing the count when a reference goes out of scope. The compiler automatically generates calls (AddRef and Release) that can be used to keep track of the number of times that an interface has been referenced. As we'll see, the "normal" way for interfaces to work is to use those compiler-generated calls to keep a count of those references. When the interface's reference count goes down to zero, then the compiler automatically frees the instance that is implementing that interface.

In this way, Delphi can do automatic memory management for interfaces. This means that once you create a class that is referenced by an interface, you can't call Free on the instance – unless you happen to have a member called Free on the interface itself. Instead, the compiler will write all the code to track the references and free the object when it is no longer referenced.

Thus, the compiler needs a way to do all that reference tracking. It also needs a way to figure out which interface is what (remember the GUID from above?). In order to do that, all classes that implement an interface need to declare and implement three methods:

```
function _AddRef: Integer; stdcall;
function _Release: Integer; stdcall;
function QueryInterface(const IID: TGUID; out Obj): HResult; stdcall;
```

These three methods are part of the root interface for all interfaces, IInterface. The first two methods are called automatically by the compiler each time it sees that a reference is used (_AddRef) and goes out of scope (_Release). The QueryInterface method is used to determine if the class implements a given interface. All three of these methods are required by the base interface IInterface and thus are required by all interfaces.

I'm not going to go into much depth here, but by now you can at least understand the declaration (and implementation) of TInterfacedObject:

```
TInterfacedObject = class(TObject, IInterface)
  protected
    FRefCount: Integer;
    function QueryInterface(const IID: TGUID; out Obj): HResult; stdcall;
    function _AddRef: Integer; stdcall;
    function _Release: Integer; stdcall;
  public
    procedure AfterConstruction; override;
    procedure BeforeDestruction; override;
    class function NewInstance: TObject; override;
    property RefCount: Integer read FRefCount;
  end;

. . .

function TInterfacedObject._AddRef: Integer;
begin
  Result := InterlockedIncrement(FRefCount);
end;

function TInterfacedObject._Release: Integer;
begin
  Result := InterlockedDecrement(FRefCount);
```

```
  if Result = 0 then
    Destroy;
end;
```

You can see the entire declaration of TInterfacedObject in the System.pas unit. It basically does all the housekeeping of managing the reference count of the implementing object, and destroying it when the count gets to zero. It should be noted, too, that referencing an interface's reference count is thread-safe because the _AddRef and _Release methods use Interlocked operations. This means that you can safely access interface implementations across multiple threads. Note that this doesn't mean that all your code is thread-safe – just that the referencing of interfaces between threads is thread-safe.

Some further things to note about using TInterfacedObject:

- If you want reference counting for your interfaces, you need to either descend your implementing classes from TInterfacedObject, or declare similar functionality in your class. The majority of your interface implementing classes will probably descend directly from TInterfacedObject.
- The RTL also provides two additional, but less commonly used, classes that implement the three "magic" interface functions. TAggregatedObject and TContainedObject are designed to be aggregated or contained by an outer, controlling class. If you have an implementing class that will create and control internal interfaces, you can use these classes as base classes and they will be reference counted and managed by their controlling, external classes.
- You should never have a need to call the three "magic" methods of TInterfacedObject. If you feel the need to, you almost certainly are doing something you shouldn't be. Pay no attention to what the IDE's code completion tells you – don't call them or mess with them in any way.
- With regard to the previous note, it is interesting that you can call the methods on TInterfacedObject in your code despite them being protected or even private in scope. Remember, they are part of the interface, and the interface doesn't have the notion of private, protected, or public.

Reference counting of interfaces also means that you should never, ever mix interface references with "real" object references to an implementing class. Never. Just don't do it – it can lead to the reference counting system being by-passed, leaving you with stranded references to objects out on the heap.

For instance, the following code mixes object and interface references:

```
procedure DoNotMixInterfaceAndObjectReferences;
var
  ObjectReference: TInterfacedObject;
  InterfaceReference: IInterface;
begin
  ObjectReference := TInterfacedObject.Create();
  // RefCount is 0
  InterfaceReference := ObjectReference;
  // RefCount is 1
  InterfaceReference := nil;
  // this causes RefCount = 0, thereby destroying the underlying object
  // but ObjectReference is still in scope and might be used.
end;
```

Again, don't do this as it is very easy to create an access violation. Keep your interface references and your object references completely away from each other and don't mix them.

2.11 How to Actually Use Interfaces

Okay, so now you know about declaring and implementing interfaces. But how do you actually **use** them? It's quite straight forward. You simply declare a variable of the interface type you want to create, and then assign to it an instance of an object that implements that interface. A simple example would look like this:

```
var
  NamedPerson: IName;

begin
    NamedPerson:= TPerson.Create;
    WriteLn(NamedPerson.FirstName, ' ', NamedPerson.LastName, ' is a person.');
end;
```

Here are some things to note about the simple example above:

- First, TPerson descends from TInterfacedObject, and therefore it meets the minimum requirements for implementing an interface – that is, _AddRef, _Release, and QueryInterface.
- NamedPerson is defined as IName. This means that you can only call the methods of IName on NamedPerson even though TPerson may have more methods than IName does.

- Because interfaces are reference counted, there is no need for a `try...finally` block with a call to `Free`. Sure, you create an object, but the compiler will keep track of all references to the instance and free it when there are no references left. The construct may look a little strange to you at first – I know that I was very used to seeing the `try...finally` block – but the resulting code is simpler and easier to manage.

Interfaces can be used anywhere that regular variables are used. You can pass them as parameters and declare them as fields, properties and local variables. Indeed, you should take advantage of interfaces everywhere you can.

2.12 Why Should You Be Using Interfaces?

Okay, so you know what interfaces are and how to use them. Now I'll say it: You should be using interfaces. All the time. Well, pretty much all the time, anyway. For pretty much everything. As much as possible. I said earlier that they are probably the single most effective tool you have in your arsenal. That's a pretty weighty statement, and I don't use it flippantly.

The what and the how are the easy part. It's not difficult to figure out how this all works. It's the *why* that seems to be the sticking point for many – I know it was for me for a long time. Why in the heck would you want to use these crazy things?

Well here's why.

Coding Against Abstractions

Interfaces allow you do something that is critical to writing good code: They allow you to program to an abstraction. A pure abstraction, in fact. Why do you want to program to abstractions and not implementations? The simple answer is this: an interface is the smallest, thinnest, and least complicated thing you can couple your code to. As discussed above, loosely coupled code is good.

Now, if your code is completely decoupled, then it can't do anything at all. Code has to be coupled to **something** in order to provide any useful functionality, so "perfectly decoupled" code is going a touch too far – what you really want is loosely coupled code. Very loosely coupled code. You want the coupling of your code to be as loose as humanly possible. If you never couple to anything but interfaces, then that is as loosely coupled as you can get.

Ultimately, this is the bottom line reason why you should use interfaces in Delphi: They provide a very thin – but very powerful – abstraction to your code. Much of the rest of this book is really an expansion on that one simple but fundamental idea. Think of your code as Lego blocks, with pins on one side and holes on the other side. With this loosely coupled interface you can join any block to every other block and create anything you want. It would be very limiting if the red blocks had a different hole size than the green blocks' pins, no?

As I've said before, and I'll say again: A good developer codes against abstractions, and not implementations. Interfaces are a great way to create abstractions. If you want a thorough discussion on why this is a good idea, I suggest reading Erich Gamma on the topic[2] – but I'll talk a bit about it here.

Pluggable Implementations

If you program against abstractions, you can't couple yourself to a specific implementation. Interfaces allow you to make the coupling between your classes very loose. Classes should be developed and tested in isolation with few or no external dependencies. But they almost certainly have to depend on something. And certainly once you have a well-designed class library created, you need to piece it together to create the system you need to build – just like a child can build almost anything he or she wants out of Lego blocks. In the end, an interface is the lightest and thinnest thing that a class can depend on. (I've likened coupling to interfaces as "grasping at smoke".) So, if you program primarily with interfaces, you can't help but create very loosely coupled code. And we all know that loosely coupled code is good. So interfaces help produce good code.

But there's more – interfaces also let you alter implementations, even at runtime. Because you are dealing with an interface, and not an implementation, you can very easily pick and choose what implementation you want when you want. For instance, you can write code like this:

```
procedure EncryptSomething(aSuperSecretStuff:TBuffer; const aIWantToBeSafe: B\
oolean);
  var
    Encryptor: IEncrypt;
  begin
    if aIWantToBeSafe then
    begin
      Encryptor := TSuperDuperPowerfulEncryption.Create;
    end else
    begin
      Encryptor := TWhoCaresHowSafe.Create;
    end;
    Encryptor.Encrypt(aSuperSecretStuff);
  end;
```

This is a silly example, but you can see how this can be very useful – you can have a single interface and select the proper implementation at runtime as needed. In fact, I'd say that if you can't choose your implementation at runtime, then your code is too tightly coupled.

A more practical example might be an ICreditCardProcessor interface where you instantiate different credit card implementations based on the choice made by your customer. Because you aren't tied to a specific implementation, you can use a single ICreditCard interface while making it easy to alter which implementation gets used. If you want to add a new credit card processor,

---

[2]http://www.artima.com/lejava/articles/designprinciples.html

it's as easy as implementing a new class and adding it to the means you use to choose the credit card processor. No changing the main code that handles credit cards – it doesn't matter what implementation you use.

And of course, you might think that your implementation of your interface is great, but it's entirely possible that a better one will come along, and you want to be able to easily plug that new implementation in without having to radically change your code. Interfaces make that quite possible and easy. A good rule of thumb is to *"Always develop against interfaces and code as if a radically better implementation is just around the corner.*[3]*"* (That sounds too good to be my original quote. I can't find it's origin, and I did try. If the quote is yours, please let me know and I'll be happy to provide proper attribution.)

Intermodule Communications

But wait, there is more! Interfaces are good for inter-module communications. Say you have a large system with different teams working on different major modules. Those teams are responsible for providing functionality in their own modules, and thus they are responsible for the integrity and quality of the code in their modules. Let's say you are on the Widget team, and you need the Sprocket team to do something for you. You go to the Sprocket guys and say "Hey, I need to add a few things in the Sprocket code so that we can do some Sprocket-type stuff in our Widget." The Sprocket guys are going to laugh at you – like they are going to let you poke around in their carefully crafted system!

No, instead, they will likely ask you what you need, build the functionality, and hand you some code with an interface and a factory for instantiating an implementation of that interface. They aren't going to let you anywhere near their code – but they are happy to let you have an interface into that code. You get what you want – some Sprocket functionality – and they don't have to expose anything more than an interface to you.

And later, if they completely re-architect their code, what do you care? Your interface still works, even if they completely change the internal implementation. That's a sound way to develop, all made possible because of interfaces.

Testable Code

It doesn't end there – interfaces make your code testable. As noted above, because you are using interfaces you can readily substitute any implementation you want. What if you are testing and you don't want to connect to the production database? You can simply provide a fake implementation for your database connection interface – one that only pretends to be the database and that returns canned data – and now you can test your code in isolation without actually connecting to a database. I'll discuss this more in the chapter on unit testing.

---

[3] https://twitter.com/NickHodges/status/146018445002145792

Patterns

Finally, interfaces make it easy to implement design patterns and do things like Dependency Injection. Most of the new patterns and practices – including Dependency Injection frameworks – are enabled because of the power and flexibility of interfaces. Development patterns and architectures such as Model-View-Controller (MVC) and Model-View-ViewModel (MVVM) are much easier to implement and use when designed with interfaces.

If you choose not to embrace interfaces, then you are locking yourself out of new and effective programming frameworks and techniques. I'll be covering Dependency Injection in depth in a later chapter, and you'll see then that without interfaces, Dependency Injection would not be as easy as it could be.

Still not convinced? I'll put it another way: all the cool kids are doing interfaces, and you want to be part of the cool kid group, right?

3 Understanding Generics

Added to the language in Delphi 2009, Generics are a powerful language feature that allow you to write type-safe classes, interfaces, arrays and even methods that act upon a "type to be named later". Sometimes you write code and you realize that you have to do a lot of type-casting to coerce something to be a specific type. Or perhaps you are writing a lot of subclasses to handle the specific case of a specific type, and you are writing a lot of duplicate code. This is where Generics come in.

A generic type is one that takes a type as a parameter, and allows you to use that type in your code without knowing ahead of time what the exact type is. (It's kind of hard to define generics without using the word 'type' all the time...). You can tell your generic type to accept any type, or you can use constraints, which will limit the types that can be passed to ones with parameterless constructors, or types of a specific class or those that implement specific interfaces.

The term "Generics" is sort of a common term for this language feature. I prefer the more formal "Parameterized Types" to describe them. Why? Well, because I think parameterized types is more accurate and descriptive. You are 'passing in' the type to the method just like you pass in regular parameters. The syntax is slightly different, but once you realize that, "parameterized types" makes more sense. However, most people call them generics, and so that is the term I'll use throughout the book. However, I won't hesitate to point out how generics really are types being passed as parameters. And besides, "generics" is easier to type.

 Most of the examples in this chapter will focus on using generics with classes, but you should note that generics work equally well with interfaces and records.

Let's start off with a simple example. Consider the following code:

```
type
  TStack = class
private
  FStack: array of Pointer;
public
  procedure Push(X: Pointer);
  function Pop: Pointer;
end;
```

This is a very simple stack declaration (We won't worry about the implementation here...). But it has a problem – it is a stack of pointers. And that's great if you want to keep a stack of raw pointers, but it becomes a bit of a problem if you want to put, say, integers or strings or something else in the stack. You can do it, but you'll have to either typecast the integers when pushing and popping, or you'll have to create a new stack specifically for integers. The former is tricky and error prone, and the latter, say:

```
type
  TIntegerStack = class
  private
    FStack: array of integer;
  public
    procedure Push(X: integer);
    function Pop: integer;
  end;
```

means that now you have two classes that you have to maintain. Create one for every type that you might want to deal with and now you have a large set of classes to deal with, and if you find a bug in your implementation, then you have to change it in all of them.

So this presents a bunch of problems. First, the two "solutions" are both tedious. The first one – the type-casting way – requires lots of specific type-casting which may seem okay, but really isn't something that you should be doing at all. In addition, it breaks the notion of encapsulation by playing fast and loose with the types being managed in a class. The other requires the creation and maintenance of a bunch of very similar classes. Plus, the work never ends, because you may come across new things that you want to store in a stack, meaning you need to create a new class for each one of them. Who wants all that?

3.1 Generics to the Rescue

A stack is a stack, right? Do we really care what kind of item is being stored in the stack? Well, no, we do not. The code is going to be the same whether you are tracking strings or TWidgets. The type doesn't matter, right? If only there was a way that we could just somehow pass in the type itself as a parameter, and then have a stack that operates on that passed-in type!

Hah! We can! That's **exactly** what generics do.

Consider this code:

```
type
  TStack<T> = class
  private
    FStack: array of T;
  public
    procedure Push(X: T);
    function Pop: T;
  end;
```

The type declaration for TStack takes a parameterized type T using angle brackets (<..>). The T represents any type at all. The code uses the T all throughout the code as if the T were the actual type. T is a convention for the variable name and is generally understood to represent 'type'. But it is just a convention – you can use any name that you like to represent the parameterized type. In addition, you can pass in as many type parameters as you wish:

```
type
  TMultipleTypes<T1, T2, T3, T4> = class;
```

There are a few things to note here:

- T can be any type at all. This can be a good thing or a problem, depending on what you want to do with T. For now, T can be anything, but later on we'll look at how you can constrain T to be a specific type or interface in order to provide more functionality.
- The type parameter T is passed to the type declaration, not to a method (although we'll see later that you can pass them to methods as well). That is where the notion of 'parameterized types' comes from. Think of the T as a parameterized type (hehe) on the main type itself, only it's being passed in using angle brackets and not regular parentheses.
- Once the T is passed in, you can use it anywhere in the class – as a variable inside a method, as a result type to a function, anywhere. Given the proper constraints, you can even create an instance of T.
- T is completely type-safe. Once the type is declared, you can't change it or use a different type than the one you declared in place for T. Once you insert a specific type for T, your declaration is type-safe and you are committed to using only that type.
- Regular polymorphic behavior applies here. If T is an interface or class type, you can pass references to descendants of T.

Using this class is really easy. Say you wanted to have a stack of buttons. You simply declare a variable:

```
var
  ButtonStack: TStack<TButton>;
```

and that is it. Now you can create an instance:

```
ButtonStack := TStack<TButton>.Create;
```

and use the ButtonStack like any other stack. The really cool thing is that TButtonStack is totally type safe – the compiler will not let you push anything into the stack except a valid TButton.

So why do you want to do this? Why use Generics? Well, there are a number of reasons:

- You can have one class that will handle any type. No more TButtonStack and TStringStack and TIntegerStack and all that. You merely have one TStack<T> to use and maintain. That is less code to worry about.
- You aren't duplicating code. This is good for many reasons, including a single point of failure and a single point to fix that failure. Having to fix the same bug in many places is inefficient, no fun, and error-prone. One class for any type is much easier to handle than many, one-type classes.
- As mentioned, you get full type safety – always a good thing. No more typecasting and type checking in your code.

One of the added benefits of the type safety of generics is that once you declare a generic type, you get full CodeInsight support for that type in the IDE.

3.2 Constraints

One of the things that you may have noticed is that since the compiler doesn't have a clue about what the type of T is, you can't do anything to T except keep track of it. You can't manipulate it or do anything to it. As noted above, if you pass in a class, you can't call any of it's methods. That's not any fun.

That's where the notion of constraints comes in. Constraints allow you to tell the compiler "I want to use a generic type here, but I want to constrain (i.e. limit) it to be a specific subset of types". By doing that, you can then call methods on the type or use the type in a known way because you've given the compiler enough information to figure out what you are doing.

The syntax for constraints is, as with most Pascal constructs, easy to understand. It consists of a colon after the parameterized type, followed by the constraint name:

```
TConstraintedType<T: constraint> = class
   ...
end;
```

A class can have multiple constraints separated by commas:

```
TConstraintedType<T: constraint1, constraint2> = class
   ...
end;
```

The things that can be used in place of `<constraint>` are discussed below.

constructor **Constraint**

The `constructor` constraint requires that the parameterized type include a simple, parameter-less constructor called `Create`. This constraint will not usually be used standing alone, but will most normally be used in conjunction with the `class` constraint as described below. Thus, the following code will compile:

```
uses
   SysUtils;

type
  TSomeClass<T: constructor> = class
    function GetType: T;
  end;

function TSomeClass<T>.GetType: T;
begin
  Result := T.Create;
end;
```

Given the above declaration, you now can create:

```
   SomeClass := TSomeClass<SomeObject>;
```

but you can't create

```
   SomeClass := TSomeClass<integer>;
```

because the `integer` type doesn't have a constructor.

`class` Constraint

The `class` constraint ensures that the type passed is – you guessed it! – a class. The `class` constraint means that the parameterized type must be a class type – that is, a `TObject` or one of it's descendants. Here is, for instance, the declaration of the `TObjectList<T>` from the `Generics.Collections.pas` unit:

```
TObjectList<T: class> = class(TList<T>)
private
  FOwnsObjects: Boolean;
protected
  procedure Notify(const Value: T; Action: TCollectionNotification); override;
public
  constructor Create(AOwnsObjects: Boolean = True); overload;
  constructor Create(const AComparer: IComparer<T>; AOwnsObjects: Boolean = Tru\
e); overload;
  constructor Create(Collection: TEnumerable<T>; AOwnsObjects: Boolean = True);\
 overload;
  property OwnsObjects: Boolean read FOwnsObjects write FOwnsObjects;
end;
```

This class specifically tracks and contains objects, so the class constraint ensures that the parameterized type accepted by `TObjectList<T: class>` is indeed a class type.

It should be noted that the `class` constraint itself is not enough to ensure that you can construct an instance of the class passed in. In fact, this code will ***not*** compile:

```
type
  TSomeClass<T: class> = class
    function GetType: T;
  end;


function TSomeClass<T>.GetType: T;
begin
  Result := T.Create; // <---- Fails here
end;
```

It produces the following compiler error:

`[dcc32 Error] ConstructorConstraint.dpr(20): E2568 Can't create new instance without CONSTRUCTOR constraint in type parameter declaration`

In order to be able to create an instance of the parameterized type, the `constructor` constraint must be included as well. Thus, the following code will compile:

```
type
  // Notice the addition of the constructor constraint
  TSomeClass<T: class, constructor> = class
    function GetType: T;
  end;


{ TSomeClass<T> }


function TSomeClass<T>.GetType: T;
begin
  Result := T.Create;
end;
```

The constructor constraint might seem redundant here, but there might be certain situations – say, when you have private constructor as with a factory class or a singleton – where you want to be able to guarantee that a default constructor is present.

record Constraint

I'm betting you can guess what the record constraint does. Yes! It constrains your type to be a record – or more specifically, a non-nullable value type.

Thus, if you have code like the following:

```
type
  TMyRecord = record
    SomeInt: Integer;
  end;


type
  TSomeClass<T: record> = class
  private
    FType: T;
  public
    constructor Create(aType: T);
    function GetType: T;
  end;


constructor TSomeClass<T>.Create(aType: T);
begin
  inherited Create;
  FType := aType;
```

```
end;

function TSomeClass<T>.GetType: T;
begin
  Result := FType;
end;

var
  SomeClass: TSomeClass<TMyRecord>;
```

You are able to declare the variable SomeClass with a TMyRecord, but if you tried to pass in a class type to TSomeClass, you'd get the following compiler error:

```
[dcc32 Error] Project44.dpr(40): E2512 Type parameter 'T' must be a non-nullable \
value type
```

interface Constraint

You can limit your parameterized types to accept only instances that implement specific interfaces. By declaring one or more interfaces (separated by commas) you declare that the type you will pass in must implement all of those interfaces. The compiler will check to make sure that your type meets the constraints. When such a constraint is met, your code can then call any of the interface's methods:

```
type
  IStoppable = interface
    procedure Stop;
  end;

  TWidget<T: IStoppable> = class
    FProcess: T;
    procedure StopProcess;
  end;

{ TWidget<T> }

procedure TWidget<T>.StopProcess;
begin
  FProcess.Stop;
end;
```

In this simple example, you can see that the TWidget<T: IStoppable> class does not care what type you pass to it, as long as it can be stopped. Thus you can create a class that accepts types that are capable of specific tasks as defined by an interface.

Passing Records as Parameterized Types

One nice feature of parameterized types is the ability to pass records as unconstrained types. Consider the following example:

```
type
  TFoo<T> = class
    AnyType: T;
  end;

  TSomeRecord = record
    procedure Blech;
  end;

  var
    Foo: TFoo<TSomeRecord>;

procedure TSomeRecord.Blech;
begin
  WriteLn('Blech!');
end;

begin
  Foo := TFoo<TSomeRecord>.Create;
  try
    Foo.AnyType.Blech;
  finally
    Foo.Free;
  end;
end.
```

Here you can see that the compiler is smart enough to recognize the type of the type parameter and allow you to call it at run-time.

3.3 Generic Interfaces

So far we've only declared generic classes. However, Delphi also allows you to add parameters to interface declarations:

```
type
  IMyInterface<T> = interface
    procedure DoSomething(aType: T);
  end;
```

This makes for a very powerful means of using generics. (I told you interfaces always make things better). Rather than constrain your parameterized type to a specific class, you can instead constrain it to a particular defined functionality – an interface – and insulate yourself from any particular implementation. (Sound familiar? I'll keep harping on that point time and time again.....)

3.4 Generic Methods

You can pass a parameterized type to the name of any method without declaring the class itself as a generic class:

```
type
  TWidgetMaker = class
  public
    function CreateWidget<T: TWidget>(aWidgetName: string): T;
  end;

...

  MyWidget := TWidgetMaker.CreateWidget<TSpecialWidget>('SpecialWidget');
```

Once you do that, the type parameter is available for use inside the method and no where else. There are some limitations to this:

- Interfaces cannot have generic methods
- Constructors, destructors, message methods and record operators cannot be generic methods.
- Properties cannot have generic methods for their getters and setters

Otherwise, you may pass parameterized types as part of a single method call. An example of this might be to pass an IComparer implementation to a method called Compare that will do the work of comparing things, allowing you to be flexible in just how that comparison gets done.

3.5 Generic Collections

Earlier I discussed a hypothetical TStack<T> which was useful because you didn't ever have to do anything with the parameterized type inside the stack. Collections like this are good, straightforward examples of how generics can be useful. And because they are useful in this way, it is no surprise that Delphi includes a set of such collections that act on any type.

> We'll cover these collections in detail in a coming chapter, but I mention them here because they are a very common use of generics in the Delphi run-time library

These collections are found in the Generics.Collections.pas unit. In addition, Spring4D has an even more extensive and powerful collections unit that we'll cover as well.

Generics.Collections contains the following generic classes for common use:

- TList<T>
- TThreadedList<T>
- TQueue<T>
- TStack<T>
- TDictionary<TKey, TValue>
- TObjectList<T>
- TObjectStack<T>
- TObjectDictionary<TKey, TValue>
- TThreadedQueue<T>

The Spring4D framework contains a unit named Spring.Collections.pas which includes a similar set of collection classes, but which are more powerful in that they all follow the IEnumerable<T> pattern. These classes will be covered more thoroughly in a coming chapter. Because of that, I won't discuss them much here, other than to point out that:

- These collections provide type-safe containers for easy use
- They provide a single class as a collection for any type, improving maintenance. One class to fix is much better than multiple classes for multiple types.
- These classes should replace the use of their non-generic counterparts (TList, TStack, etc.). You don't have to do this right away, but you should gradually replace your existing use of the regular, non-generic collection classes and their descendants with the new, generic-based ones.

3.6 Thinking Generically

So far we have looked at the "consuming" side of generics. Things like `TList<T>` are all very useful classes, and our code is made much simpler, easier to maintain, and more type-safe because of them. But using them merely makes us ***consumers*** of generics. If we want to truly take advantage of generics, we need to become ***producers*** of generic classes. It's a big step to see the benefit of generic collections, but the truly big step is to start seeing opportunities for the use of generics in your own code.

3.7 A Contrived, Simple Example

So in order to start thinking about generics with a producer's mindset, consider the following code:

```
type

  TOrderItem = class
    ID: integer;
  end;

  TOrder = class
    ID: integer;
  end;

  TCustomer = class
    ID: TGUID;
  end;
```

Now this code is very simple – a set of classes that might represent a basic order entry system. But right away, something should occur to you. All three have something in common – they are entities in your system. Down the road, you may want to act upon all the entities in your system, so you might create a superclass like so:

```
type

  TEntity = class
  end;

  TOrderItem = class(TEntity)
    ID: integer;
  end;

  TOrder = class(TEntity)
    ID: integer;
  end;

  TCustomer = class(TEntity)
    ID: TGUID;
  end;
```

However, you might be frustrated because you want your TEntity class to have an ID field that is in use by all descendants, but that pesky TCustomer class can't oblige – it needs a GUID for its ID tag instead of an integer like the other classes. And there might be other entities that need different types of ID tags.

Instead of fretting about those different types of ID tags, how about just create one that doesn't care what type it is? Well, this is where the power of generics comes in. How about you give the TEntity class a parameterized type – a generic – as its ID, and then just tell all the classes what type their ID tag will be?

```
type

  TEntity<T> = class
    ID: T;
  end;

  TOrderItem = class(TEntity<integer>)
  end;

  TOrder = class(TEntity<integer>)
  end;

  TCustomer = class(TEntity<TGUID>)
  end;
```

Now, given the above, your entities can all have ID's, but you don't have to have the same type for all of them. If a TEntity descendant needs an ID of a different type, you can just descend from

TEntity and pass the correct ID type in the class declaration.

Again, the example is quite contrived, but I think it does a nice job of showing how you can start "thinking generically" and not just accept a rigid type structure.

In addition, it illustrates why the more formal name for generics is "parameterized types". The type in the brackets is passed in to the type declaration, and then used within the class, just as method parameters are passed in to functions and procedures.

A simple, contrived example, sure. But hopefully it illustrates how generics can be used to turn you from a consumer of generic classes to making them a common tool in your code.

3.8 A Practical Example

While you will see generics used throughout the rest of the book, a straight-forward practical example is in order here. So often the simple example you see is TList<T> which is useful, but almost too simple. Above, I encouraged you to "Think Generically", and so here's an example of doing just that. It also has the added advantage of being useful.

TEnum

Enumerations are cool, and sometimes it is cool to get the string value for an enumeration. But who wants the hassle of using the TypInfo.pas unit and trying to figure that all out. How about, instead, we come up with a nice little record that wraps that all up for us while illustrating how methods can take parameterized types just like classes can?

Consider the following code:

```
uses
    TypInfo;

type
  TEnum = record
  public
    class function AsString<T>(aEnum: T): string; static;
    class function AsInteger<T>(aEnum: T): Integer; static;
  end;

class function TEnum.AsString<T>(aEnum: T): string;
begin
  Result := GetEnumName(TypeInfo(T), AsInteger(aEnum));
end;
```

```
class function TEnum.AsInteger<T>(aEnum: T): Integer;
begin
  case Sizeof(T) of
    1: Result := pByte(@aEnum)^;
    2: Result := pWord(@aEnum)^;
    4: Result := pCardinal(@aEnum)^;
  end;
end;
```

This code uses generics to allow you to find out the string and integer value of any enumerated type. Here is an example of it in use:

```
program EnumDemo;

{$APPTYPE CONSOLE}

uses
  SysUtils;

type
  TNick = (Blah, Yech, Floo);

begin
    WriteLn(TEnum.AsString<TNick>(Blah));  // writes 'Blah'
    WriteLn(TEnum.AsString<TNick>(Yech));  // writes 'Yech'
     WriteLn(TEnum.AsString<TNick>(Floo));  // writes 'Floo'

    WriteLn(TEnum.AsInteger<TNick>(Blah));  // writes 0
    WriteLn(TEnum.AsInteger<TNick>(Yech));  // writes 1
     WriteLn(TEnum.AsInteger<TNick>(Floo));  // writes 2

  ReadLn;
end.
```

Here are some things to note about the above code:

- TEnum is a record with only class methods. It contains two functions:
    - The AsString<T> function uses the simple GetEnumName call from TypInfo.pas. It returns a string value for the enumerated value. Note that it uses the AsInteger function to retrieve its result.
    - The AsInteger<T> function is a bit more complicated. Because the compiler can treat enumerated types as different integer types, the code must determine which specific integer type the value is based on its size.

- This record really is just a simple wrapper around the function `GetEnumName` from `Typinfo.pas`. Its power comes from the use of generics. Because each of the methods takes a parameterized type, you can use any enumeration with it.
- Unfortunately, there is no generic constraint that limits the passed type to be an enumeration. As a result, you can pass any type at all to `TEnum<T>`, so be careful.
- The very simple demo application merely creates a simple enumerated type, and then displays the string and integer values for each of its three items. It is nothing fancy, but illustrates how to use the record.
- Since this is just demonstration code, there is no error handling in the event of a non-enumerated type being passed to `TEnum` methods. There is no constraint that requires you pass an enumeration, so there is no way to protect against that at compile time. The record constraint can be used to constrain the types passed somewhat, but adding such error handling is left as an exercise for the reader.

Problems with Generics

Generics are a powerful and useful tool, but there are a few issues with them in Delphi.

First, they tend to drastically increase the amount of code that the compiler generates. Every time you declare a generic type, the compiler creates a new and separate type.

For instance, if you declare

```
var
  FirstIntegerList: TList<integer>;
  SecondIntegerList: TList<integer>;
```

the compiler creates two separate types. One would wish that the same type could be used internally, but currently such is not the case.

The second area where Delphi's generics may be a problem is that they don't support covariance and contravariance

Covariance is the notion that a given type can be converted from a specific type to a more general type. (Example: Corvettes can be substituted for Cars). That is, you can use a child class in place of a parent class because the child class has everything that the parent class has.

Likewise, contravariance is the notion that the general type can be substituted for the specific type. (Example, a car can replace a Corvette) Contravariance is a little trickier, and normally not allowed in object-oriented systems, because a child class can have more functionality than a parent class, and thus a parent class cannot be a perfect substitute for the child class if the child instance uses that additional functionality.

Delphi doesn't support either contravariance or covariance with generic types. This means that the following code won't compile:

```
program CovarianceExample;

{$APPTYPE CONSOLE}

uses
  System.SysUtils,
  Generics.Collections;

  Type
    TParent = class
      procedure Foo;
    end;

    TChild = class(TParent)
      procedure Bar;
    end;

procedure TChild.Bar;
begin
  WriteLn('Bar');
end;

procedure TParent.Foo;
begin
  WriteLn('Foo');
end;

var
  ParentList: TList<TParent>;

begin
  ParentList := TList<TChild>.Create;    // <--- Will not compile
end.
```

3.9 Conclusion

That is a simple introduction to parameterized types, or generics. You'll see the use of generics all throughout the rest of this book, so this chapter was designed to make you familiar with them. Generics are a powerful language feature indeed, as you will soon see.

3.10 An Interview with Generics

Nick: Generics – thanks for being with us today.

Generics: Yeah, whatever. Usually people aren't too interested in talking to me. I pretty much don't care what goes on, so I'm usually really boring.

Nick: Well, I'll bet we can find something interesting to talk about. So, what's your deal? Why are you in the language?

Generics: That's just it – as I said, I don't care what goes on around me. I'm a type that can be anything. I really don't care.

Nick: So why is that good?

Generics: Because I can provide functionality that doesn't care what the type being acted on is. You can design me to work with anything. Whatever. I don't care.

Nick: Well, don't be so hard on yourself.

Generics: Yeah, hey, well, when you have no purpose in and of yourself, it can be tough on your self-esteem, you know?

Nick: But you are such a great team player! Team you up with another type and you really have something.

Generics: That's true enough. You instantiate me with a specific type, and I really come alive! `TList<T>` looks about as boring as it gets, but `TList<TButton>`? That's something, I guess.

4 Understanding Anonymous Methods

4.1 Introduction

When I speak to Delphi developers about anonymous methods, many are at least aware of their existence, but almost no one uses them. That's too bad. Anonymous methods are a powerful and flexible way to make your code pluggable, expandable, and adaptable. They can cause you to look at your code from different perspectives. This chapter will introduce you to the notion of anonymous methods and provide a few examples of their use. By the end of this chapter, I hope that you are scheming of ways to integrate anonymous methods into your code.

4.2 Definition

You're probably not going to believe this, but an anonymous method is a method without – yes – a name. It is a "chunk" of code that stands alone without being attached to any class or even any specific named procedure. You can declare the code to stand alone, as a variable, and even pass them around as parameters to other methods.

Why are they anonymous? Well, it's a bit strange, but they are anonymous so that you can give them a name at the right time. They can be given a name when they are declared as variables or parameters. And since they don't have a name, they can't be arbitrarily called elsewhere. No one can come along and go "Oh, hey, there's a method I can use" and start altering the scope of a method by using it in places where it doesn't belong. By being anonymous, such methods are naturally limited in scope. And limiting scope is good.

Here is an example of an excessively simple anonymous method:

```
procedure(const aString: string)
begin
  WriteLn(aString);
end
```

There are a few things to notice here:

First, a quick word on syntax. Anonymous methods have syntax similar to regular methods, but with two differences. The most obvious is that they don't have a name. That's not surprising, given that they are called Anonymous Methods.

Second, you are probably thinking that I made a typo up there, because I didn't put a semicolon at the end of parameter declaration or at the anonymous method itself. Well, think again! Anonymous methods don't have semicolons at their end and they don't have one before the begin of the main body. Like all other language statements, they are stand-alone elements that have no semicolon in and of themselves.

Now, you'll often see a semicolon at the end, but that's because they are the last part of a complete statement, such as when you assign an anonymous method to a variable of the proper type and the semicolon is there to separate statements. Now I know that every ounce of your being, as a true Delphi developer, is screaming out for a semi-colon at the end of that anonymous method, but I assure you that you shouldn't put one there.

In order to declare an anonymous method, you must first declare its type. That is done by declaring a type name followed by a reference to the signature of the method to be used. For example, the type declaration for the above anonymous method would be:

```
type
  TOutputProc = reference to procedure(const aString: string);
```

That would enable you to declare a variable of type TOutputProc:

```
var
  OutputProc:   TOutputProc;
```

And then you can assign the anonymous method above to such a variable if you want:

```
OutputProc := procedure(const aString: string)
                        begin
                  WriteLn(aString);
        end;
```

And now you are saying "Aha! You do put a semi-colon at the end of anonymous methods!" Well, no. The semi-colon is there to terminate the assignment.

Don't believe me? Okay, look at the following code:

```
procedure ProcessASprocket(aSprocket: Tsprocket; Reporter: TOutputProc;)
begin
  VerifyTheSprocket(aSprocket);
  EnterSprocketInDatabase(aSprocket);
  Reporter(aSpocket.Name + ' has been processed');
end;
```

You could then call the above regular method like so:

```
ProcessASprocket(MySprocket, procedure(const aString: string)
                        begin
                          WriteEntryInLoggingTool(aString);
                        end);
```

See? The semi-colon goes on the outside of the closing parenthesis.

One further thing to note is how anonymous methods are invoked. Above I mentioned about how all anonymous methods eventually do get a name. In the case above, the `ProcessASprocket` procedure has a parameter named `Reporter` that takes an anonymous method type. At this point, then, you've assigned a name in the local scope to the anonymous method, and thus you can call it as above:

```
Reporter('This is a string');
```

4.3 Why?

If you aren't already familiar with anonymous methods, you are probably at this point asking, "Why in the world would you ever want to do something like that – it just looks like a more complicated way to do what I'm already doing?" That's understandable – they are a bit complex. But their use will, as I mentioned above, start you thinking about your code in new, interesting and powerful ways.

A Simple Example

First, they can be used to define a method signature that your code can call, but that can be defined later. This enables you to define a class that is open to additional functionality at run-time by consumers of that class. Here's an example.

Let's say you want to create a simple calculator. You might do it like this:

```
type
  TCalculator = class
    function Add(x, y: integer): integer;
    function Subtract(x, y: integer): integer;
  end;
```

```
...
```

```
function TCalculator.Add(x, y: integer): integer;
begin
  Result := x + y;
end;
```

```
function TCalculator.Subtract(x, y: integer): integer;
begin
  Result := x - y;
end;
```

Now, this is a pretty straight forward class. But its functionality is fixed, and you can't do anything to it except Add and Subtract. That is it. If you want to multiply, you are out of luck. You have to either add functionality to the class or descend from it and extend its functionality using inheritance.

Either way, you as the developer of the code have to do that. If you are trying to build a framework that others might want to use, they'd have to alter your framework or use inheritance to make it do things that they might want it to do, too.

But what if there were a way to provide the ability to extend this class at run-time? What if you could provide a way for other developers to do other types of calculations without them having to alter your class? What if someone thinks up a much, much better way to do addition that is so cool that they want to replace your lame addition algorithm with theirs?

Have you guessed yet that anonymous methods let you do all of that and more? Sure you have.

Okay, so take a look at this calculator class:

```
TIntegerFunction = reference to function(const x, y: integer): integer;

TIntegerCalculator = class
strict private
  FList: IDictionary<string, TIntegerFunction>;
  procedure RegisterOperators;
public
  constructor Create;
  procedure RegisterMathOperator(aName: string; aCalculation: TIntegerFunction);
  function Calculate(aName: string; x, y: integer): integer;
```

```
end;

...

function TIntegerCalculator.Calculate(aName: string; x, y: integer): integer;
begin
  Result := FList[aName](x, y);
end;

constructor TIntegerCalculator.Create;
begin
  inherited;
  FList := TDictionary<string, TIntegerFunction>.Create;
  RegisterOperators;
end;

procedure TintegerCalculator.RegisterOperators;
begin
  RegisterMathOperator('Add', function(x, y: integer): integer
                                 begin
                                          Result := x + y;
                                 end);
  RegisterMathOperator('Subtract', function(x, y: integer): integer
                                 begin
                                          Result := x - y;
                                 end);

RegisterMathOperator('Multiply', function(x, y: integer): integer
    begin
      Result := x * y;
    end);
end;

procedure TIntegerCalculator.RegisterMathOperator(aName: string;
      aCalculation: TIntegerFunction);
begin
  FList.Add(aName, aCalculation);
end;
```

Okay, so this looks kind of complicated for a calculator. And it is more complicated than the first demo, but it is of course more capable. Now, you have a class that can do any kind of calculation on a pair of integers as long as you define and register the function that does it by name. Internally, it registers three mathematical operations, but of course, anyone using the class can add any type of calculation that they want. For instance, one only need add the following to include a Power function:

```
function Power(x, y: integer): integer;
begin
  if y = 0 then
  begin
    Result := 1;
  end else
  begin
    Result := x * Power(x, y - 1);
  end;
end;


...


MyCalculator.RegisterMathOperator('Power', function(x, y: integer): integer
                                  begin
                                    Result := Power(x, y);
                                  end  );
```

Here are some things to note about the above code:

- By adding the Power function, you've extended the capabilities of the class without altering it, and provided a way for the consumers of your code to provide their own implementations and methods without having to change your class. In fact, the class doesn't do anything but provide that capability, really.
- And in case you haven't noticed, that means that your class is following the SOLID[1] principle of leaving your class open for extension but closed for modification (i.e., the Open/Closed Principle).
- The functions themselves were passed as literals. That is, the method parameter called for an anonymous method type, and that code was literally entered right into the method call.
- Anonymous methods are called as you would expect – by the local name, with any parameters required passed as parameters normally are.
- Note as well that the implementation of a specific anonymous method must match the declaration of the anonymous method type. All anonymous methods must be defined before they can be declared.

---

[1]http://butunclebob.com/ArticleS.UncleBob.PrinciplesOfOod

Anonymous Methods as Variables

Above we saw anonymous methods being passed as literals. You can also assign code to a variable and then pass that variable around like any other. The `RegisterMathCalculation` might be called like this:

```
var
  SubtractCalc: TIntegerFunction;
begin
  SubtractCalc := function(x, y: integer): integer
                            begin
                              Result := x - y;
                  end);
  RegisterMathCalculation('Subtract', SubtractCalc);
end;
```

In this way, you can treat blocks of code like variables.

4.4 Closures

By now, you may be saying "Why should I use anonymous methods? I've been doing exactly this with method pointers for years.". Okay, fair enough. But anonymous methods provide a powerful feature not supported by mere method pointers – closures.

A closure is the notion that an anonymous method can capture or "close around" the state of the method within which they are called. Anonymous methods can reference and thus capture local variables outside of their specific scope but within the scope in which they are called. In this way, they are similar to nested functions but are more flexible because they can be called from outside the scope where they are defined. They will not just capture local variables, but all variables seen in the current scope, including any variables declared by the object where the anonymous method resides.

Keeping with our arithmetic theme, here is a very simple demo of a closure occurring in a method:

```
unit ClosureDemo;

interface

type
  TSingleInteger = reference to procedure(x: integer);

  procedure DoStuff;

implementation

procedure DoStuff;
var
  a: integer;
  b: integer;
  AddFive: TSingleInteger;
begin
  b := 5;
  AddFive := procedure(x: integer)
             begin
               WriteLn(x + b);
             end;

  for a := 1 to 10 do
  begin
    AddFive(a);
  end;
end;

end.
```

This is a very simple example, but it shows what closures do. In this case, a local variable b exists outside the scope of the AddFive procedure, but b is still available and "captured" inside the anonymous method. In this way, anonymous methods can participate in the greater scope of a method in which they are contained. If AddFive were to be passed out of the DoStuff procedure, the value for b would go right along into the remote call despite being outside the scope of AddFive. It should be noted that these variables are captured by reference and not by value.

4.5 Standard Declarations

The Delphi Runtime Library (RTL) declares a number of anonymous procedure and function types that are "standard" fare for your use in your code. These declarations save you the trouble of declaring your own types and ensure that a common set of types are used throughout a module. These declarations are found in the System.SysUtils.pas unit.

The first is a series of procedures that take up to four parameters:

```
type
  TProc = reference to procedure;
  TProc<T> = reference to procedure (Arg1: T);
  TProc<T1,T2> = reference to procedure (Arg1: T1; Arg2: T2);
  TProc<T1,T2,T3> = reference to procedure (Arg1: T1; Arg2: T2; Arg3: T3);
  TProc<T1,T2,T3,T4> = reference to procedure (Arg1: T1; Arg2: T2; Arg3: T3; Arg4\
: T4);
```

Notice, of course, that these are parameterized types, allowing the arguments to be of any type that you want. So for instance, if you want to declare an anonymous procedure that takes a string and a double as parameters, you can declare:

```
var
  StringDoubleProc: TProc<string, double>;
begin
  StringDoubleProc := procedure(aString: string; aDouble: Double)
                      begin
                        ShowMessage(aString + ' ' + FloatToStr(aDouble));
                      end;
end;
```

The RTL provides declarations for up to four parameters. You can declare your own if you need more than four, but at that point you might consider refactoring to not require so many parameters.

There are also standard declarations for functions:

```
TFunc<TResult> = reference to function: TResult;
TFunc<T,TResult> = reference to function (Arg1: T): TResult;
TFunc<T1,T2,TResult> = reference to function (Arg1: T1; Arg2: T2): TResult;
TFunc<T1,T2,T3,TResult> = reference to function (Arg1: T1; Arg2: T2; Arg3: T3): T\
Result;
TFunc<T1,T2,T3,T4,TResult> = reference to function (Arg1: T1; Arg2: T2; Arg3: T3;\
 Arg4: T4): TResult;
```

These are declared in a similar manner to the procedures, only because they are functions, they include a parameterized type that defines the return type for the function. Thus, you can do the following:

```
function AddIntegers(a, b: integer): integer;
var
  AddFunc: TFunc<integer, integer, integer>;
begin
  AddFunc := function(x, y: integer): integer
              begin
                Result := x + y;
              end;
  Result := AddFunc(a, b);
end;
```

4.6 A Practical Example

One way in which anonymous methods are useful is by simplifying code for common coding patterns.

For instance, the following code pattern is probably familiar and common:

```
begin
  OldCursor := GetCurrentCursor;
  try
    Cursor := crHourglass;
    // Do some lengthy process that makes you want to show the hourglass cursor
  finally
    Cursor := OldCursor
  end;
end;
```

Well, this kind of construct is screaming out for an anonymous method:

```
procedure ShowHourGlass(Proc: TProc);
var
  OldCursor: TCursor;
begin
  OldCursor := Screen.Cursor;
  Screen.Cursor := crHourGlass;
  try
    Proc;
  finally
    Screen.Cursor := OldCursor
  end;
end;
```

Then, you can call it like so:

```
ShowHourGlass( procedure
               var
                 i: integer;
               begin
                 for i := 1 to 99999999 do;
               end);
```

The result is fewer lines of code and a common way to display the hour glass cursor in all instances. I'm sure you can find other similar patterns in your code where anonymous methods might prove useful. For instance, if you do threading code, I bet you have a lot of try...finally blocks with locks, TMonitor, and critical sections that are ripe for using anonymous methods.

4.7 Another, Cooler Example

The C# guys love to brag about their cool using feature. It's sort of like a combination of Delphi's with and try...finally statements. It defines a particular scope which, when left, will automatically dispose of the object in question. Delphi doesn't have this specific language construct, but by combining anonymous methods and generics, we can provide the same functionality:

```
Obj = class
  class procedure Using<T: class>(O: T; Proc: TProc<T>); static;
end;

class procedure Obj.Using<T>(O: T; Proc: TProc<T>);
begin
  try
    Proc(O);
  finally
    O.Free;
  end;
end;
```

This is basically a (sorry) generic way of wrapping up try...finally blocks just like we did with the cursor above. You can use it like so:

```
Obj.Using<TStringList>(TStringList.Create, procedure (List: TStringList)
begin
  List.Add('One');
  List.Add('Two');
  List.Add('Three');
  List.Add('Four');
  ListBox1.Items := List;
end);
```

This is another good example of using a coding pattern with an anonymous method to make coding a little easier. In this case, the Obj.Using enables you to set the items in a listbox in a single step. It can be useful for a small, short-lived object that you need to do something within a single method. You might want to consider using this technique anytime you create a variable on the stack.

Now I have to be honest and point out that I have taken this example directly from Allen Bauer's blog[2].

Anonymous Methods are very flexible

Since the very beginning, Delphi has had a strong event-driven model. Methods could be declared with the of object syntax and then they could be assigned object methods to run when called. A typical event declaration looks like this:

```
type
  TNotifyEvent = procedure(Sender: TObject) of object;
```

then, you could declare a method – and it had to be a method of an object – of type TNotifyEvent and assign it to a variable of that type.

```
property OnClick: TNotifyEvent read FOnClick write FOnClick
```

Then, your code could call the variable when the event is fired:

```
    procedure DoOnClick;
    begin
      if Assigned(FOnClick) then FOnClick(Self);
    end;
```

Where do anonymous methods enter into things here? If you declare a variable as an anonymous method, you can assign to that variable an anonymous method (of course), a method reference, and even a regular old stand-alone procedure. This means that you can declare your event types as anonymous methods, and then have great flexibility in what kind of code you can assign to those methods.

Consider the following code:

---

[2]http://blogs.embarcadero.com/abauer/2008/09/25/38870

```pascal
program AssignAnyProcToAnonMethods;

{$APPTYPE CONSOLE}

uses
    System.SysUtils
  ;

type
  TMethodReference = procedure(aString: string) of object;
  TAnonMethod = reference to procedure(aString: string);
  TProcReference = procedure(aString: string);

var
  AM: TAnonMethod;
  PR: TProcReference;

  procedure ProcReference(aString: string);
  begin
    WriteLn('I am a Procedure Reference: ' + aString);
  end;

type
  TSomeClass = class
  private
    FEvent: TAnonMethod;

  public
    procedure MethodReference(aString: string);
    procedure SetMethodReference(aAnonReference: TAnonMethod);
    constructor Create;
    procedure FireEvent;
    property OnEvent: TAnonMethod read FEvent write FEvent;
  end;

var
  SomeClass: TSomeClass;

constructor TSomeClass.Create;
begin
  inherited;
  FEvent := MethodReference;
```

```pascal
end;

procedure TSomeClass.FireEvent;
begin
  if Assigned(FEvent) then
    FEvent('Firing Event');
end;

procedure TSomeClass.MethodReference(aString: string);
begin
  WriteLn('I am a Method Reference: ' + aString);
end;

procedure TSomeClass.SetMethodReference(aAnonReference: TAnonMethod);
begin
  FEvent := aAnonReference;
end;

begin
    PR := ProcReference;

    AM := procedure(aString: string)
          begin
            WriteLn('I am an Anonymous Method: ' + aString);
          end;

    SomeClass := TSomeClass.Create;
    try
      SomeClass.SetMethodReference(AM);
      SomeClass.FireEvent;
      SomeClass.SetMethodReference(PR);
      SomeClass.FireEvent;
      SomeClass.SetMethodReference(SomeClass.MethodReference);
      SomeClass.FireEvent;
    finally
      SomeClass.Free;
    end;
  ReadLn;
end.
```

Here are some things to note about the above code:

- Instead of declaring the event as of object which is typical in the Delphi RTL and VCL, it declares the event as an anonymous method using reference to.
- The OnEvent event is then assigned three different types of routines, all which have the same signature: a stand-alone procedure, a method reference, and an anonymous method. All three are assigned and then run, showing that you can assign any of the three to an anonymous method reference.
- This code illustrates that going forward, you should strongly consider declaring all of your event types as anonymous methods, which will give you more flexibility in implementing your events.

4.8 Anonymous methods in the RTL

The Run-time Library in Delphi XE has begun to take advantage of anonymous methods.

TThread and Anonymous Methods

Just as above, where the using construct provides a means of using a small, discreet type that needs to perform a task within the local scope, you may have a small discreet chunk of code that you want to run in a separate thread.

First, there is the CreateAnonymousThread method:

```
class function CreateAnonymousThread(const ThreadProc: TProc): TThread; static;
```

that will create a thread from your anonymous method. The thread is created suspended, so you can call start on it as you please. It is also created with FreeOnTerminate set to True, so once you start the thread, you should "forget" about it and let it run. Again, this can be used as a "fire and forget" thread for a discrete, small chunk of code that you want to run in a separate thread.

Next, if you need to ensure that your code needs to be synchronized with the rest of your application (perhaps because it calls VCL code.....) then you can use this overloaded version of Queue:

```
class procedure Queue(AThread: TThread; AThreadProc: TThreadProcedure); overload;\
  static;
```

to call code using TThread's synchronization logic with an anonymous method.

4.9 Predicates

What is a predicate you ask? Well, it's simple. A predicate is a specific type of function that takes a single parameter and returns a Boolean value. It is basically a reference to a method (usually an anonymous method) that is tied to a type that it takes as a parameter and returns either True or False. That's it. Told you it was simple.

Okay, I guess there is more to it than that. Most commonly, a predicate will take the form of an anonymous method. The Delphi RTL declares the following type:

```
TPredicate<T> = reference to function (Arg1: T): Boolean;
```

Thus, a predicate is a generic type that takes the parameterized type as a single argument and returns a Boolean result. Just like I said.

So What?

By now you are probably asking "So what?" Well, TPredicate allows you to declare things like this:

```
var
  IsLessThan10: TPredicate<integer>;
begin
  IsLessThan10 := function(const aValue: integer): Boolean
                  begin
                    Result := aValue < 10;
                  end;
  ...
end;
```

Now you have a nice compact, portable way to determine if a number is less than ten. You can pass that around to methods and use it to determine if a number is greater or less than ten.

```
procedure CheckIsLessThan10;
var
  IsLessThan10: TPredicate<integer>;
  i: integer;
begin
  IsLessThan10 := function(const aValue: integer): Boolean
                  begin
                    Result := aValue < 10;
                  end;
```

```
  Write('Enter an integer: ');
  Readln(i);

  if IsLessThan10(i) then
  begin
    Writeln(i, ' is LESS THAN 10');
  end else
  begin
    Writeln(i, ' is GREATER THAN OR EQUAL to 10');
  end;
end;
```

So your next question is "Why use an anonymous method? Why not just use a regular function?"

Well, predicates can be an elegant replacement for if statements. Not for every if statement, but for some. For instance, a predicate can answer the question "Should I include you or not?" on each item in a list of items.

Let's say that your Boss comes to you and asks you to give him all the numbers from one to 100 that are evenly divisible by seven. You might write your code like this:

```
procedure IsDivisibleBy7;
var
  i: Integer;
begin
  for i := 1 to 100 do
  begin
    if i mod 7 = 0 then
    begin
      Write(i, ', ');
    end;
  end;
  WriteLn;
end;
```

And that will work great. No sweat.

Your boss loves the results, but then he comes and says "Hey, how about a list of numbers that are less than 25 and divisible by two?" You say sure, and then you work up a procedure called IsLessThan25, but as you are writing it, you realize that there's a pattern here – and that your boss is probably going to keep asking for things like this.

You're lazy, and you don't want to keep writing the same routine over and over again with only minor changes. You know that could become a maintenance nightmare. And then you see the pattern – the only thing that will change is the boolean statement that you are using. Predicates to the rescue!

```
procedure OutputMatchingNumbers(aIsQualified: TPredicate<integer>);
var
  i: Integer;
begin
  for i := 1 to 100 do
  begin
    if aIsQualified(i) then
    begin
      Write(i, ', ');
    end;
  end;
  WriteLn;
end;
```

And here's the program for your Boss:

```
procedure DoOutputMatchingNumbers;
var
  IsDivisibleBy7: TPredicate<integer>;
  IsLessThan25DivBy2: TPredicate<integer>;
begin

  IsDivisibleBy7 := function(const aInteger: integer): Boolean
                          begin
                            Result := aInteger mod 7 = 0;
                          end;
  OutputMatchingNumbers(IsDivisibleBy7);

  IsLessThan25DivBy2:= function(const aInteger: integer): Boolean
                           begin
                             Result := (aInteger < 25) and (aInteger mod 2 = 0);
                           end;
  OutputMatchingNumbers(IsLessThan25DivBy2);

end;
```

Now, when your Boss comes and asks for another output, it becomes nothing more than adding another predicate and calling it using your standalone function. And who knows what kind of stuff your boss is going to ask for, right? You have a template and a simple function for doing exactly what he wants, over and over again. And not only that, because the solution involves an anonymous method, you have a re-usable algorithm in case another system requires such a predicate.

Okay, so that was a pretty simple yet illustrative example. By now you should at least have a basic idea of how predicates work. In the coming chapters, you'll see a more practical application for them, similar to what we saw above – similar but more useful.

4.10 Conclusion

That's a brief overview of anonymous methods. You'll see them again along with generics in some of the later chapters. This powerful feature enables a lot of cool new constructs and interesting techniques. The Delphi Spring Framework will make use of them as will the new DUnitX Unit Testing Framework.

4.11 An Interview with Anonymous Methods

Nick: Anonymous Methods, you are a hard guy to find!

AM: Yes, I am. I like it that way.

Nick: Well, I appreciate you taking the time to answer my questions, even if it is only over IM.

AM: Yeah, no problem. You'll never figure out who I am anyway.

Nick: Indeed – so what is up with this whole "no name" thing anyway? How is anyone supposed to call you?

AM: Well, I don't have a name for a reason. If I had a name you could call me anywhere! We can't have that! Because I don't have a name, I can only be called in the exact places where my type is asked for. This gives me a lot of power despite the limitation of not having a name.

Nick: Like what? What can you do that a named method can't?

AM: Well, for starters, I can be assigned to a variable. If you declare a variable of my type, say `TFunc<T, TResult>`, then you can pass me around just like any other variable. Watch:

```
MyAdditionFunction := function(a, b: integer) begin Result := a + b; end;
```

Sweet, huh?

Nick: That could be interesting.

AM: Yeah, it sure is, particularly when you consider I also take advantage of Closures.

Nick: Closures?

AM: Yeah – wherever I am, I can "close" around all the variables that are in my scope, and those variables go with me wherever you send me. That can be useful and powerful.

Nick: Yeah, I can see that. What other advantages do you have because you are anonymous?

AM: Well, you can pass me directly as a parameter. No kidding. Like this:

```
begin
  ProcessAWidget(procedure(aWidget, aWidgetProcessor) begin aWidgetProcessor.Proc\
essWidget(aWidget) end);
end;
```

Let's see one of those named routines do **that**! Hoo Hoo Hoo!

Nick: Whoa – settle down, now. So basically, because you have no name, you can act like a variable.

AM: Yeah, that's pretty much right. The trick is that you just have to define my type via a specific signature before hand. Then, you can provide any number of instances of code for that particular type, and go to town.

Nick: And what does that mean?

AM: Well, it means that you don't have to formally declare all kinds of methods. It means you can easily choose among different implementations at run-time based on a simple variable name. For instance, you can create a thread and execute me all in one step – no need to even create a thread.

Nick: Whoa, huh?

AM: Yeah, TThread has a new class function that does that. Booyah! Try that easily with a named method!

Nick: That is cool.

AM: Damn skippy it is.

Nick: Hey, thanks for stopping by – this is good information.

AM: Yeah, you're welcome. Just don't tell anyone who I am.

5 Delphi Collections

5.1 Introduction

Delphi developers should be very familiar with collections, though the term itself can be misleading. We've all used some type of data structure to hold on to a bunch of similar items, whether it be an array, a `TList`, or some other similar structure.

However, with the advent of parameterized types as well as the `for...in` statement, the types of collections and the things that those collections can do have improved dramatically. In fact, the generics-based collections are so powerful and preferable, that we won't even discuss the non-parameterized collection types in Delphi. This chapter will cover the basics of those collections and how you can use them to improve your code quality.

> The term "collection" is a bit overloaded. In the general sense, it is used to describe any data structure that is meant to hold and maintain elements of a given type or interface. Lists, stacks, queues, dictionaries and a bevy of other more complex structures are all collectively called "collections." However, with Delphi "collection" is itself a specific type of container – that is, one which contains items in no specific order. I will endeavor to be clear about my usage of the word.

In this chapter, we'll discuss two sets of collections: those provided by Delphi out of the box in the `Generics.Collections` unit, as well as the collections that come with the Delphi Spring Framework.

5.2 General Notions about Collections

There are many types of collections. Below is a table covering the most common types of collections and how they differ:

Collection Type	Description/Discussion
Collection	A Collection is a group of items in no particular order. In computer science terms, they are often referred to as a "bag". You can't insert items into a specific location in a collection, only add or remove them. A collection can't be sorted because it has no order.
List	A list is a group of items in a particular order. Items can be sorted and inserted at any index position in the list. Lists are array-like. Their elements are numbered from zero and have a specific index which can be used to find each item.

Collection Type	Description/Discussion
Dictionary	A dictionary is a data structure that allows you to "look up" items. Items in the structure have both a key and a value. A particular value can be found by looking it up using its associated key. With Delphi's dictionary, the key can be of any type (it doesn't have to be a string as in other languages) and the value can be of any type too.
Stack	A stack is a "First In, Last Out" data structure. Think of a spring-loaded stack of plates at the cafeteria – you "push" plates onto the stack, and then "pop" them off in reverse order.
Queue	A queue is a First In, First Out data structure. Think of an ordinary line that you wait in, or a tube in which items are inserted at one end and taken out on the other.

These are the only collections we'll discuss here, as they are the ones provided by both the `Generics.Collections` unit and the Delphi Spring Framework.

5.3 The Delphi-Provided Collections

Delphi includes a unit called `System.Generics.Collections`. In it is a set of generic collections that you can easily use in place of the traditional collections that you've used in the past. It contains the following types:

- `TList<T>`
- `TQueue<T>`
- `TStack<T>`
- `TDictionary<TKey, TValue>`

In addition, there are descendant classes that can manage the lifetime of the objects that they contain:

- `TObjectList<T>`
- `TObjectQueue<T>`
- `TObjectStack<T>`
- `TObjectDictionary<TKey, TValue>`

Further, there are two types that handle their items via threading:

- `TThreadList<T>`
- `TThreadedQueue<T>`

All of these collections, with the exception of `TThreadList` and `TThreadedQueue` are able to be used with Delphi's `for...in` syntax. (The "why" and "how" of this will be discussed below.)

TList<T>

TList<T> is probably the most commonly used of all the collections. As noted above, it is a collection that provides indexing, insertion, deletion, exchanging, searching, and sorting. Because it is generic, it can keep track of literally any type that you want, while remaining completely type safe. It probably will become the "workhorse" of your collections arsenal.

Here is a simple example that shows the basics of what TList<T> can do:

```
unit uListDemo;

interface

procedure DemoList;

implementation

uses
    Generics.Collections
  ;

type
  TIntegerList = TList<integer>;

procedure OutputList(aMessage: string; aIntegerList: TIntegerList);
var
  i: integer;
begin
    Write(aMessage, ', the list is: ');
    for i in aIntegerList do
    begin
      Write(i, ', ');
    end;
    WriteLn;
end;

procedure DemoList;
var
  IntegerList: TIntegerList;
  Temp: Integer;
  i: integer;
begin
  IntegerList := TIntegerList.Create;
```

```
  try
    for Temp := 1 to 10 do
    begin
      IntegerList.Add(Temp);
    end;
    OutputList('At the start', IntegerList);

    for i in IntegerList  do
    begin
      if i mod 2 = 0 then
      begin
        IntegerList.Remove(i);
      end;
    end;
    OutputList('After removing even numbers', IntegerList);

    // Insert 42 where the evens were
    for Temp := 1 to 9 do
    begin
      if Temp mod 2 = 0 then
      begin
        IntegerList.Insert(Temp, 42);
      end;
    end;
    OutputList('After inserting 42', IntegerList);

    IntegerList.Sort;
    OutputList('After sorting', IntegerList);
  finally
    IntegerList.Free;
  end;
end;

end.
```

As you can see, the list can be manipulated in almost any way you want. The demo above illustrates how you can easily create a list of integers without having to declare a completely separate class each time, and without any type-casting.

TStack<T>

Delphi's collections also include `TStack<T>`, which provides the normal functionality of this classic data structure. You can push items onto the stack and pop them off in a Last In, First Out (LIFO) manner. A stack is often illustrated by the spring-loaded stack of plates at a cafeteria, where you "push" plates down onto the stack of plates, and customers "pop" them off the top in the reverse order that they were put in.

Interestingly, a fun test of a stack is to see if it can detect palindromes. A palindrome is a word, phrase or any sequence of letters that reads the same forwards and backwards. Since a stack pushes things in one direction and then pops them off in reverse order, a stack can be used to detect if a given string is a palindrome.

```pascal
unit uStackDemo;

interface

function IsPalindrome(const aString: string): Boolean;

implementation

uses
        Generics.Collections
    , System.SysUtils
    , Character
    ;

type
  TCharStack = TStack<Char>;

function IsPalindrome(const aString: string): Boolean;
var
  Stack: TCharStack;
  C: Char;
  TempStr: string;
  i: integer;
  CharOnly: string;
begin
  Stack := TCharStack.Create;
  try
    for C in aString do
    begin
      if TCharacter.IsLetter(C) then
        Stack.Push(TCharacter.ToLower(C));
    end;

    TempStr := '';
```

```
    for i := 0 to Stack.Count - 1 do
    begin
      TempStr := TempStr + Stack.Pop;
    end;

    CharOnly := '';
    for C in aString do
    begin
      if TCharacter.IsLetter(C) then
        CharOnly := CharOnly + C.ToLower;
    end;
    Result := TempStr = CharOnly;
  finally
    Stack.Free;
  end;
end;

end.
```

This code demonstrates the basic functionality of `TStack<T>`. Each individual character of the given string is "pushed" down onto the stack, and then they are "popped" off in reverse order.

In addition, the class provides the ability to `Peek` at the next item on the stack without removing it. And of course, being a parameterized collection, it can contain elements of any single type with full type safety.

5.4 TQueue<T>

`TQueue<T>` is similar to a stack, but instead of a LIFO process, it uses a FIFO process, "First In, First Out". I like to think of it as a tube where you put golf balls in one end and then let them roll through to the other end. The first golf ball you put in is the first one that comes out the other end, and the rest "wait their turn" to come out after the first ones.

A common use for queues is to hold on to tasks that are yet to be done. A simple demo might be to track maintenance requests at an apartment building. There might be any number of requests that come in for things to be fixed, and to be fair, you want to fix them in the order that they are received. Thus, a very simple system might look something like this:

```
unit uQueueDemo;

interface

uses
      Generics.Collections
    ;

type
  TWorkOrder = record
    Description: string;
    constructor Create(aDescription: string);
  end;

  TWorkOrderQueue = TQueue<TWorkOrder>;

procedure DoRepairs;

implementation

procedure DoWorkOrder(aWorkOrder: TWorkOrder);
begin
  WriteLn('I am now doing this job: ', aWorkOrder.Description);
end;

procedure DoRepairs;
var
   WorkOrderQueue: TWorkOrderQueue;
  i: Integer;
begin
  WorkOrderQueue := TWorkOrderQueue.Create;
  try
    // Orders come in
    WorkOrderQueue.Enqueue(TWorkOrder.Create('Fix the sink in #543'));
    WorkOrderQueue.Enqueue(TWorkOrder.Create('Repair air conditioner in #156'\
));

    //Time for one item
    DoWorkOrder(WorkOrderQueue.Dequeue);

    // More orders come in!
    WorkOrderQueue.Enqueue(TWorkOrder.Create('Stock the public bathroom'));
```

```delphi
    WorkOrderQueue.Enqueue(TWorkOrder.Create('Fix door handle on #307'));
    WorkOrderQueue.Enqueue(TWorkOrder.Create('Catch mouse in #124'));
    WorkOrderQueue.Enqueue(TWorkOrder.Create('Repair the refrigerator in #402\
'));

    // I can squeeze one in!
    DoWorkOrder(WorkOrderQueue.Dequeue);

    // More work!!!
    WorkOrderQueue.Enqueue(TWorkOrder.Create('Unplug toilet in #109'));
    WorkOrderQueue.Enqueue(TWorkOrder.Create('Repair Carpet in #405'));
    WorkOrderQueue.Enqueue(TWorkOrder.Create('Replace bathroom doorknob in #3\
22'));
    WorkOrderQueue.Enqueue(TWorkOrder.Create('Repair air conditioner in #143'\
));

    // All right, let's finish them all

    while not WorkOrderQueue.IsEmpty
    begin
      DoWorkOrder(WorkOrderQueue.Dequeue);
    end;

  finally
    WorkOrderQueue.Free;
  end;
end;


{ TWorkOrder }

constructor TWorkOrder.Create(aDescription: string);
begin
  Description := aDescription;
end;

end.
```

This simple example shows how a queue can be used to line things up for later use.

TDictionary<TKey, TValue>

TDictionary<TKey, TValue> is a powerful collection type. It is a container that stores key/value pairs, such that you can retrieve a value by using its key to search for it. Its strength lies in the fact that it is a generic type and that both the key and the value can be of any type at all. For instance, you could have a dictionary that had a TLabel as the key and a TButton as the value.

For a simple example, we'll create a TDictionary<string, double> that will track student's grade point averages (GPA). In it, we can add students with their GPAs, look those GPAs up, and then change them.

```
unit uDictionaryDemo;

interface

uses
    Generics.Collections
  ;

type

  TStudentGPADictionary = TDictionary<string, double>;

procedure ProcessStudents;

implementation

uses
    System.SysUtils
  ;

procedure ReportOnStudents(aStudents: TStudentGPADictionary);
var
  Student: string;
begin
  for Student in aStudents.Keys do
  begin
    WriteLn(Student, ' has a ', Format('%.2f', [aStudents[Student]]), ' GPA.'\
);
  end;
end;

procedure ProcessStudents;
```

```
var
  StudentGPADictionary: TStudentGPADictionary;
begin
  StudentGPADictionary := TStudentGPADictionary.Create;
  try
    // Add some students
    StudentGPADictionary.Add('Sally Superstar', 4.0);
    StudentGPADictionary.Add('Harry Hardworker', 3.73);
    StudentGPADictionary.Add('Andy Average', 2.55);
    StudentGPADictionary.Add('Freddy Failure', 1.01);

    // Report out on students
    ReportOnStudents(StudentGPADictionary );
    WriteLn;

    WriteLn('Oops, we miscalculated!....');
    StudentGPADictionary['Andy Average'] := 2.62;
    StudentGPADictionary['Harry Hardworker'] := 3.70;
    // Report out on students
    ReportOnStudents(StudentGPADictionary );
    WriteLn;
  finally
    StudentGPADictionary.Free;
  end;
end;

end.
```

Some things to note:

- Items in a dictionary are not stored in any particular order.
- Enumerating over the items will not necessarily produce them in the same order in which they were entered.

Object Collections

All of the collections above have descendants that allow you to manage objects (i.e., TObjectList<T>, TObjectStack<T>, TObjectQueue<T>, and TObjectDictionary<TKey, TValue>. These classes behave exactly like their parents, except they are specifically designed to contain objects. You can, via the constructor or the OwnsObjects property, tell the container that it is the owner of the contained classes – that is, when the OwnsObjects property is True, the container is responsible for freeing the objects it contains. If OwnsObjects is False, then TObjectList<T> is basically the same as 'TList

5.5 Collections in the Delphi Spring Framework

The `Spring.Collections` unit in the Delphi Spring Framework contains a similar set of functionality as does `Generics.Collections`, but it is more powerful and flexible in a number of significant ways.

The collections classes in Spring4D are similar enough and perform basically the same as the ones in the Delphi RTL that I won't spend a lot of time covering the specifics. I will however, highlight some of the differences and additional capabilities provided by Spring4D.

General Discussion

The Collections in Spring4D are all accessible through the `Spring.Collections` unit. The various collections themselves are implemented in other units, but you should never need to use them. Why? Because `Spring.Collections` defines a set of interfaces that give you access to all the functionality of the other units. All the collections in Spring4D are accessed via interfaces, making them more flexible and easier to use than classes.

Further, the collections can all be created by a factory class called `TCollections`, which is a collection of `class` methods that return implementations of the various collections. This class will provide instances for most of the collection types that you will need. If you do need to create a collection with a specific constructor, you can add the specific implementing units to your project and call them from that unit. However, you should always access the Spring4D collections via their interfaces.

For instance, if you want to create an `IQueue<T>`, all you need to do is the following:

```
var
  MyQueue: IQueue<string>
begin
  MyQueue := TCollections.CreateQueue<string>;
  ...
end;
```

Spring4D provides the following collection interfaces:

Non-generic collections:

- ICollection
- IList
- IDictionary
- IStack
- IQueue
- ISet

These types are useful in that they can contain `TValue` types – a variant-like data structure that is part of the new Delphi RTTI.

In addition, Spring4D has these generic collections that can hold any type:

- `ICollection<T>`
- `IList<T>`
- `IDictionary<T>`
- `IStack<T>`
- `IQueue<T>`
- `ISet<T>`

Of course, Spring4D also provides complete implementations of these classes as well as easy access to those implementations via the `TCollections` factory.

These interfaces behave in the same general way as their counterpart classes in the Delphi RTL, with one big exception – the `IEnumerable<T>` interface. In Spring4D, `IEnumerable<T>` is a very powerful, feature-rich interface that is implemented by all the generic collections in Spring4D. `IEnumerable<T>` is so cool that I'll devote a whole chapter to it.

Two Collection Types Not Yet Covered

Spring4D has two collection types that aren't found in the set of Delphi generic collection types – `ICollection<T>` and `ISet<T>`.

`ICollection<T>` is the most basic collection type there is – it merely contains items in no particular order. I've seen this collection type called a "bag" or a "bucket" before. All you can do is `Add` and `Remove` items from the collection, as well as iterate over all of them. That's it – no sorting, ordering, inserting at specific locations or any of the other things that a `List` will do. The only way to get at the items is by enumerating them.

`ISet<T>` is probably what you'd expect – a set-like collection that allows you to determine and create relationships between two collections. `ISet<T>` descends from `ICollection<T>` and adds the ability to treat collections as sets. You can determine the union and intersection of two collections, as well as whether the two collections overlap or not. You can merge two collections together or create a new collection that is the intersection of the two.

5.6 Why you should be using the Spring4D Collections

I recommend that you use the collections in the `Spring.Collections.pas` unit instead of the ones that come with the Delphi RTL. I do so for the following reasons:

- The Spring4D collections are interface-based and are thus easier to manage in your code.
- They all implement Spring4D's `IEnumerable<T>`. As we'll see in the next chapter, this is a powerful interface for managing, iterating, and using collections.
- They provide two collections that are not provided by the Delphi RTL – ICollection and ISet.

5.7 Conclusion

Collection classes are a common and necessary part of development. When combined with generics and interfaces, they become a very powerful coding tool. In the next two chapters we'll see ways to make collections even more powerful by using enumeration and `IEnumerable<T>`

6 Enumerators in Delphi

6.1 Introduction

I've talked about how these collections can work with Delphi's `for...in` syntax. But how do you make your own classes work with the `for...in` statement?

Well, it's pretty easy. In order to do so, you need to provide these four things.

1. A class or record that will enumerate within `for...in` must provide a function called `GetEnumerator()`.
2. The `GetEnumerator` function must return a class, record, or implemented interface that has the following:
3. A method called `MoveNext` that returns a `Boolean` indicating whether the end of the collection has been reached or not
4. A read-only property called `Current` that indicates the item that is currently being "looked at" as the enumeration occurs.

That's a bit convoluted, so at this point a simple demo would be helpful, no?

You can already enumerate the characters in a string, but it's a simple example, and so how about we create an enumerator that runs through the characters in a string?

```
TForInDemoClassEnumerator = class
  private
    FString: string;
    FIndex: integer;
  protected
    function GetCurrent: Char; virtual;
  public
    constructor Create(aString: string);
    function MoveNext: Boolean;
    property Current: Char read GetCurrent;
  end;

TForInDemo = class
  private
    FTheString: string;
```

```
    procedure SetTheString(const Value: string);
  public
    constructor Create(aString: string);
    function GetEnumerator: TForInDemoClassEnumerator;
    property TheString: string read FTheString write SetTheString;
  end;
```

This code declares two classes. The first class is the enumerator – the class that does the work of moving over each item, and which will be returned by the call to GetEnumerator. The second is the class that will be enumerated. Notice, too, that TForInDemoClassEnumerator has the read-only property Current with the reader GetCurrent and MoveNext methods. The TForInDemo class has a call to GetEnumerator that returns an instance of TForInDemoClassEnumerator.

First let's look at TForInDemoClassEnumerator. You create it by passing the constructor the item to be enumerated – in this case a string. Hence, the constructor:

```
  constructor Create(aString: string);
```

Here is the implementation of the MoveNext method:

```
  function TForInDemoClassEnumerator.MoveNext: Boolean;
  begin
    Result := FIndex < FString.Length;
    if Result then
    begin
      Inc(FIndex);
    end;
  end;
```

This code does two things. First, it sets the result. The function returns True if the enumerator is able to move to the next item, and False if it has reached the end of the items to be enumerated. In this case, it merely checks to see the index is before the length of the string. If the end has not yet been reached, it just increases the FIndex field. So its job is to move the index along, and report if the end has been reached.

The actual item itself is returned by the GetCurrent method, which is self-explanatory:

```
  function TForInDemoClassEnumerator.GetCurrent: Char;
  begin
    Result := FString[FIndex];
  end;
```

One thing that should be noted is that MoveNext is called before the Current property is accessed for the first time. This can trip you up and cause off-by-one errors if you aren't aware of this. Be very careful when implementing your enumerators, as it is easy to make a mistake.

And that is it for the enumerator. It's pretty simple. But we'll soon see that you can do some cool things with these enumerators because you have complete control over how they return the data that they are enumerating over.

The next step is to see how the actual class to be enumerated provides its enumerator to the compiler. When the compiler builds the for...in loop construct, it looks at the in part of the construct and thinks "Hey, I need an enumerator here, so I'll call GetEnumerator". If the item in question indeed has a method called GetEnumerator, it calls it, and all is well. If not, the compiler raises an error because the type in the in part of the for...in loop isn't able to be enumerated.

But of course, our TForInDemo class has such a method, and it is quite simple:

```
function TForInDemo.GetEnumerator: TForInDemoClassEnumerator;
begin
  Result := TForInDemoClassEnumerator.Create(FTheString);
end;
```

It merely creates and returns an instance of our enumerator, passing it the string value it is storing for the purpose of enumerating. Pretty easy and straight-forward, really.

Now that we've created all these classes, you can run the following code:

```
procedure DoStuff;
var
  ForInDemo: TForInDemo;
  C: Char;
begin
  ForInDemo := TForInDemo.Create('HelloWorld');;
  try
    for C in ForInDemo do
    begin
      Write(C, ',');
    end;
    WriteLn;

  finally
    ForInDemo.Free;
  end;
end;
```

6.2 IEnumerator<T> Interface

Now, the above discussion talks a lot about specific methods that must be included as part of an enumerator and as part of a class that wants to be enumerated. And of course, that should immediately make you think "Interfaces!" And sure enough, there are some nice interfaces that fall out of this (You knew I'd work interfaces into things here eventually, didn't you? Yes, you did.).

Consider this interface:

```
type
  IEnumerator<T> = interface
  ['{DD445F01-975D-405E-BCC1-09D3E78CB0FF}']
    function GetCurrent: T;
    function MoveNext: Boolean;
    property Current: T read GetCurrent;
  end;
```

That should look awfully familiar. It's the exact two methods and one property needed to implement an enumerator – hence the name.

I've declared this IEnumerator<T> interface myself, but the Delphi RTL includes a similar one in the System.pas unit. And at its base, IEnumerable<T> is all about implementing the GetEnumerator method.

It leverages generics because the type of what is being enumerated doesn't matter as far as the interface is concerned. And remember when I said that a call to GetEnumerator could return an interface? Well it can, and the compiler will happily use an IEnumerator<T> to implement the for...in loop.

Thus, your enumerators can implement this interface and your calls to GetEnumerator can return this interface, and you can add flexibility to how they are implemented. Here's an example:

```
TStringEnumerator = class(TInterfacedObject, IEnumerator<Char>)
private
  FIndex: integer;
  FString: string;
  function GetCurrent: Char;
public
  constructor Create(aString: string);
  function MoveNext: Boolean;
  property Current: Char read GetCurrent;
end;

TInterfaceEnumeratorDemo = class
```

```
private
  FTheString: string;
  procedure SetTheString(const Value: string);
public
  constructor Create(aString: string);
  function GetEnumerator: IEnumerator<Char>;
  property TheString: string read FTheString write SetTheString;
end;
```

Notice that the call to GetEnumerator returns an IEnumerator<Char> which is actually the individual type being iterated. In this case, the generic type needs to be the same type as the variable being returned in the for part of the for...in loop.

This enables you to do the following:

```
procedure DoInterfaceStuff;
var
  InterfacedEnumerator: TInterfaceEnumeratorDemo;
  c: Char;
begin
  InterfacedEnumerator := TInterfaceEnumeratorDemo.Create('GoodbyeWorld');
  try
    for c in InterfacedEnumerator do
    begin
      Write(C, ',');
    end;
    WriteLn;
  finally
    InterfacedEnumerator.Free;
  end;
end;
```

6.3 Specialized Enumerators

The implementation of an enumerator is, as I mentioned, really simple. But what if you wanted to get a little creative in the GetCurrent method? After all, at that point you have complete control over what the enumerator returns. In our simple case with characters and strings, what if we decided to, say, always return the uppercase version of the character? Or if we were iterating over integers, return the squares of the numbers in the collection? That would be super easy, right? Well, yes, it would.

Consider this code:

```
TForInDemoClassUpperCaseEnumerator = class(TForInDemoClassEnumerator)
protected
  function GetCurrent: Char; override;
end;
```

```
    ...
```

```
function TForInDemoClassUpperCaseEnumerator.GetCurrent: Char;
begin
  Result := UpCase(inherited GetCurrent);
end;
```

This class descends from TForInDemoClassEnumerator and overrides the existing enumerator for our demo class and returns the uppercase of the character in question.

If we wanted, we could return this class from our GetEnumerator call, but that would be sort of playing a trick on the user of our code. How about if we provide two different enumerators, and then make each available for enumeration in a for...in loop. Surely that is possible, right? Of course it is.

First, we'll look at the end result and then work our way backwards to see how it was implemented, because you have to play a little trick to expose more than one enumerator for a class:

```
procedure DoMoreStuff;
var
  C: Char;
  ForInExtraDemo: TForInDemoExtraIterators;
begin

  ForInExtraDemo := TForInDemoExtraIterators.Create('Greetings');
  try
    for C in ForInExtraDemo.AsUpperCase do
    begin
      Write(C, ',');
    end;
    WriteLn;
end;
```

This little routine will display the string "Greetings" as G,R,E,E,T,I,N,G,S in the console. But note in the for...in loop that the actual class is not passed to the in clause, but a method that returns a "proxy" class that has the desired enumerator attached to it instead. This is implemented as follows:

```
TUpperCaseEnumeratorProxy = class
  private
    FOwner: TForInDemo;
  public
    constructor Create(aOwner: TForInDemo);
    function GetEnumerator: TForInDemoClassUpperCaseEnumerator;
  end;
..
constructor TUpperCaseEnumeratorProxy.Create(aOwner: TForInDemo);
begin
  inherited Create;
  FOwner := aOwner
end;

function TUpperCaseEnumeratorProxy.GetEnumerator: TForInDemoClassUpperCaseEnum\
erator;
begin
  Result := TForInDemoClassUpperCaseEnumerator.Create(FOwner.TheString);
end;
```

This is just another class that can be enumerated – it has a call to GetEnumerator – and thus be returned by a method call on our "real" enumerating class. It returns an instance of an enumerator called TForInDemoClassUpperCaseEnumerator which we looked at above. So, if you want to iterate over the upper case version of the strings, you call it as we did in the DoMoreStuff method above. The trick here is that instead of iterating over the class itself, you iterate over the proxy class using ForInExtraDemo.AsUpperCase. It's a neat little trick, eh?

Thus, the enumerating class becomes:

```
TForInDemoExtraIterators = class(TForInDemo)
private
  FUpper: TUpperCaseEnumeratorProxy;
public
  constructor Create(aString: string);
  property AsUpperCase: TUpperCaseEnumeratorProxy read FUpper;
end;
...
constructor TForInDemoExtraIterators.Create(aString: string);
begin
  inherited Create(aString);
  FUpper := TUpperCaseEnumeratorProxy.Create(Self);
end;
```

So, that should give you a little insight into what happens with for...in loops and how you can create classes that participate automatically. As you can see, there is some power there, and in the rest of this chapter and the next, we'll be building on this principle to look at some interesting uses of this ability to enumerate.

6.4 TEnumerable<T> in Generics.Collections

All of the collections above descend from a class called TEnumerator<T>. In the Delphi RTL, TEnumerator<T> is an abstract class that defines two methods that needs to be overridden, namely DoGetCurrent and DoMoveNext. What each does should be self-explanatory based on what we've seen in this chapter. Each of the generic collections has a nested type called TEnumerator that overrides and implements these methods.

Similar to what we just did in the previous section, DoGetEnumerator returns an instance of TEnumerator<T> which in turn defines the methods needed for an enumerator. Those methods are DoCurrent, which gets the current item and returns it via the Current property, and MoveNext, which returns a boolean that indicates whether or not the enumerator was able to move to the next item. Thus, as a result of descending from TEnumerable<T>, the non-threaded collections are usable with Delphi's for...in syntax.

> Note that an enumerator doesn't guarantee that the items will be returned in any given order, just that every item will be returned once.

6.5 Conclusion

Enumerators are a powerful tool to use with your collections. They enable you to control access to the elements of a collection and to retrieve them out of the collection under your own terms.

7 IEnumerable

In the Collections chapter, I talked about the Spring4D collections, and how they all implement IEnumerable<T>. This interface and its implementation is so cool that it requires its own chapter.

Normally, one of the common things that you'll want to do with a collection is to iterate over the contained items in search of a specific subset. Sometimes you want the first five of them. Sometimes you want all the even ones, or all the items that start with 'k'.

For instance, let's say you have a collection of integers, and you want to find out which one of them is the biggest. The classic solution has usually been something like this:

```
program ListEnumerableDemo;

{$APPTYPE CONSOLE}

uses
    System.SysUtils
  , Spring.Collections;

var
  List: IList<Integer>;
  i, Biggest: integer;
begin
    List := TCollections.CreateList<integer>;
    List.AddRange([1,6,2,9,54,3,2,7,9,1]);

    Biggest := MaxInt -1;
    for i := 0 to List.Count - 1 do
    begin
      if List[i] > Biggest then
      begin
        Biggest := List[i];
      end;
    end;
    WriteLn('The biggest is: ', Biggest);
end.
```

That's really conventional, and will certainly get the job done. But in this day and age, that's the "old-fashioned" way to do it. Wouldn't it be so much more fun to do it in one line of code, like this:

```
program ListEnumerableDemo;

{$APPTYPE CONSOLE}

uses
    System.SysUtils
  , Spring.Collections;

var
  List: IList<Integer>;

begin
    List := TCollections.CreateList<integer>;
    List.AddRange([1,6,2,9,5487,3,2,7,9,1]);

    WriteLn(List.Max);
    ReadLn;
end.
```

Now that is how you find something in a collection. There doesn't even appear to be any looping going on at all. Obviously somewhere the list is being iterated over, but it's all been abstracted away for you. You want the maximum value to be found in the list? Just ask for it. Cool.

The key part above, of course, is the use of two things. First, the IList<T> – an interface to a generic list – and secondly, the IEnumerable<T> which descends from IEnumerable. Both are defined in the Spring.Collections unit.

> Again, I should point out that this entire chapter is based on the collections unit of the Spring4D framework. While the Delphi RTL contains a set of generic collections, they are much more limited in functionality than what Spring4D provides. It's implementation of IEnumerable<T> for instance, is much more powerful and complete – and closer to what .Net provides.

7.1 IEnumerable<T>

Those of you who also use .Net are probably familiar with IEnumerable<T> already, but perhaps you didn't know that much of the same power was available to you in your Delphi code. For those of you not familiar, you are in for a treat.

The IEnumerable<T> interface is implemented by all of the classes discussed in the previous chapter, and so any of them can be accessed as an IEnumerable<T>. Here is the declaration of IEnumerable<T>:

```
IEnumerable<T> = interface(IEnumerable)
  function GetEnumerator: IEnumerator<T>;
  function AsObject: TObject;
  function TryGetFirst(out value: T): Boolean;
  function TryGetLast(out value: T): Boolean;
  function First: T; overload;
  function First(const predicate: TPredicate<T>): T; overload;
  function FirstOrDefault: T; overload;
  function FirstOrDefault(const defaultValue: T): T; overload;
  function FirstOrDefault(const predicate: TPredicate<T>): T; overload;
  function Last: T; overload;
  function Last(const predicate: TPredicate<T>): T; overload;
  function LastOrDefault: T; overload;
  function LastOrDefault(const defaultValue: T): T; overload;
  function LastOrDefault(const predicate: TPredicate<T>): T; overload;
  function Single: T; overload;
  function Single(const predicate: TPredicate<T>): T; overload;
  function SingleOrDefault: T; overload;
  function SingleOrDefault(const predicate: TPredicate<T>): T; overload;
  function ElementAt(index: Integer): T;
  function ElementAtOrDefault(index: Integer): T;
  function All(const predicate: TPredicate<T>): Boolean;
  function Any(const predicate: TPredicate<T>): Boolean;
  function Contains(const item: T): Boolean; overload;
  function Contains(const item: T; const comparer: IEqualityComparer<T>): Boolean\
; overload;
  function Min: T;
  function Max: T;
  function Where(const predicate: TPredicate<T>): IEnumerable<T>;
  function Skip(count: Integer): IEnumerable<T>;
  function SkipWhile(const predicate: TPredicate<T>): IEnumerable<T>; overload;
  function SkipWhile(const predicate: TFunc<T, Integer, Boolean>): IEnumerable<T>\
; overload;
  function Take(count: Integer): IEnumerable<T>;
  function TakeWhile(const predicate: TPredicate<T>): IEnumerable<T>; overload;
  function TakeWhile(const predicate: TFunc<T, Integer, Boolean>): IEnumerable<T>\
; overload;
  function Concat(const collection: IEnumerable<T>): IEnumerable<T>;
  function Reversed: IEnumerable<T>;
  procedure ForEach(const action: TAction<T>); overload;
  procedure ForEach(const action: TActionProc<T>); overload;
  procedure ForEach(const action: TActionMethod<T>); overload;
```

```
  function EqualsTo(const collection: IEnumerable<T>): Boolean; overload;
  function EqualsTo(const collection: IEnumerable<T>; const comparer: IEqualityCo\
mparer<T>):    Boolean; overload;
  function ToArray: TArray<T>;
  function ToList: IList<T>;
  function ToSet: ISet<T>;
  function GetCount: Integer;
  function GetIsEmpty: Boolean;
  property Count: Integer read GetCount;
  property IsEmpty: Boolean read GetIsEmpty;
end;
```

That's a lot of cool stuff, right? Many of the methods here are pretty clear – it's pretty obvious what the Min and Max methods do. But some of the others are a bit trickier. You can get all of the items. You can get the First and Last items. You can get the first "x" number of items. You can get the items back out as a List, an Array, or a Set. And most powerfully, you can get any particular group of the items using a predicate.

7.2 Predicates

Remember our humble little predicates from a previous chapter? The anonymous method type declared as:

```
TPredicate<T> = reference to function(const value: T): Boolean;
```

Well, they are about to become really important and useful. IEnumerable<T> uses them frequently and effectively. Remember the example of "included or not?" Well, that's what IEnumerable<T> is really good at. It holds an iteration of things. You pass a predicate, and it can determine if you want the items to be part of the result or not. If the predicate is True, then the individual item is "in", or included. If it is "out", then the predicate will return False, or excluded. So if you want to get all the items in a list strings that contain the letter 'z', then you can do the following:

```
function ContainsLetterZ: IEnumerable<string>;
var
  List: IList<string>;
begin
  List := TCollections.CreateList<string>;
  List.AddRange(['zoo', 'park', 'city', 'town', 'museum', 'jazz festival']);

  Result := List.Where(function(const aString: string): Boolean
                  begin
                    Result := aString.Contains('z');
                  end);
end;
```

The above uses the Where method to determine items that should be returned as part of a new IEnumerable<string>. The above is saying "return to me an enumerable item where all the strings in the list have 'z' in them."

You can do similar things with the TakeWhile method, which returns items from the start of the list as long as the predicate is True, and stops once the predicate is False. You can determine if a given container has or doesn't have a given element. You can Skip over a given number of elements and take the rest. You can use a predicate to SkipWhile a certain thing is true, and then return the rest once the predicate returns True. Basically, once you have a reference to a collection or any IEnumerable<T> instance, you can get out of it pretty much anything you want using predicates.

Another nice feature here is that many of the functions in IEnumerable<T> return an IEnumerable<T>, enabling you to chain them together if you like, such as:

```
for Element in List.Skip(1).Take(10) do...
```

You can even combine them with predicates to return desired values. For instance, the following code returns the first even number in a given list:

```
List.Where(function(Num: Integer)
        begin
          Result := Num mod 2 = 0;
        end).First();
```

Here is a simple table that describes what each of the methods of IEnumerable<T> does. When I refer to "the collection" in this table, I'm referring to the collection that is represented by the instance of IEnumerable<T>.

Method	Description
`function GetEnumerator: IEnumerator<T>;`	Returns the enumerator for the collection in case you want to enumerate the items yourself.
`function AsObject: TObject;`	Returns an instance to the collection itself.
`function TryGetFirst(out value: T): Boolean;`	Returns `True` if the first item in the collection can be found, and `False` if it cannot. The item itself is returned in the out parameter.
`function TryGetLast(out value: T): Boolean;`	Same as `TryGetFirst`, only for the last item in the collection
`function First: T; overload;`	Returns the first item in the collection.
`function First(const predicate: TPredicate<T>): T; overload;`	Returns the first item in the collection that causes the predicate to return `True`.
`function FirstOrDefault: T; overload;`	Returns the first value found in the collection, or the default value if nothing is found. The `Default` value is the one returned by the `Default()` function for the given type. This is a "compiler magic" function that basically returns a "zero memory" value for the type (i.e., zero for numbers, and empty string, or nil.
`function FirstOrDefault(const defaultValue: T): T; overload;`	Returns the first item found in the collection or the default value that you specify
`function FirstOrDefault(const predicate: TPredicate<T>): T; overload;`	Returns the first item found that causes the predicate to return `True`. If none are found, then the `Default` value is returned.
`function Last: T; overload;` `function Last(const predicate: TPredicate<T>): T; overload;,` `function LastOrDefault(const defaultValue: T): T; overload;` `function LastOrDefault(const defaultValue: T): T; overload;`	The same as the `First` methods, only for the Last item in the collection
`function Single: T; overload;,` `function Single(const predicate: TPredicate<T>): T; overload;` `function SingleOrDefault: T; overload; function SingleOrDefault(const predicate: TPredicate<T>): T; overload;`	Returns the only element in the collection (or the default value). If the collection has more than one element, an exception is raised.

Method	Description
`function ElementAt(index: Integer): T; function ElementAtOrDefault(index: Integer): T;`	Returns the item at a specific index (or the default value)
`function All(const predicate: TPredicate<T>): Boolean; function Any(const predicate: TPredicate<T>): Boolean; function Contains(const item: T): Boolean; overload; function Contains(const item: T; const comparer: IEqualityComparer<T>): Boolean; overload;`	Return True if every element in the collection satisfies the predicate. Returns True if any of the elements in the collection satisfy the predicate. Determines if a given collection contains a specific item, using either the default comparer or one which you provide.
`function Min: T; function Max: T;`	Returns the minimum and maximum values in the collection.
`function Where(const predicate: TPredicate<T>): IEnumerable<T>;`	Returns an IEnumerable<T> that contains all the items in the collection that match the criteria of the predicate
`function Skip(count: Integer): IEnumerable<T>`	Skips over the first count items in the collection, and then returns an IEnumerable<T> containing the rest.
`function SkipWhile(const predicate: TPredicate<T>): IEnumerable<T>; overload;`	Skips over items until it reaches one that satisfies the predicate, and then returns an IEnumerable<T> containing the remaining items.
`function Take(count: Integer): IEnumerable<T>;`	Returns the first count items in the collection.
`function TakeWhile(const predicate: TPredicate<T>): IEnumerable<T>; overload;`	Returns items as IEnumerable<T> from the beginning of the collection until the predicate is False.
`function Concat(const collection: IEnumerable<T>): IEnumerable<T>;`	Returns the two given collections as a single 'IEnumerable
`function Reversed: IEnumerable<T>;`	Returns the items in the collection in reverse order
`procedure ForEach(const action: TAction<T>); overload; procedure ForEach(const action: TActionProc<T>); overload;`	Performs a given action on each item in the collection.
`function EqualsTo(const collection: IEnumerable<T>): Boolean; overload function EqualsTo(const collection: IEnumerable<T>; const comparer: IEqualityComparer<T>): Boolean; overload;`	Determines whether the two collections are equal, using either the default comparer or a comparer that you provide.

Method	Description
`function ToArray: TArray<T>;` `function ToList: IList<T>; function ToSet: ISet<T>;`	Returns the collection as an `Array<T>`, an `IList<T>`, or an `ISet<T>`
`property Count: Integer read GetCount;`	Returns the total number of items in the collection.
`property IsEmpty: Boolean read GetIsEmpty;`	Returns `True` if the collection is empty, and `False` otherwise.

The code for this book includes an example application that illustrates the use of most of the items in the table above. That code can be found as part of `IEnumerableExample.dproj` at:

https://bitbucket.org/NickHodges/nickdemocode/[1]

If you consider it for a moment, you can see that that `IEnumerable<T>` is really the root of the LINQ[a] feature of .Net. One way to view LINQ is that LINQ statements are parsed, turned into a predicate, and run against a collection, whether that collection originates in a database or a list or XML.

[a]http://msdn.microsoft.com/en-us/library/vstudio/bb397926.aspx

Something to consider: If you have a nicely composed class that includes a private `IList<T>` which gets exposed through proxy methods, then you might want to expose access to the items via a property of type `IEnumerable<T>` instead of exposing the actual list itself.

The real power of `IEnumerable<T>` is shown with the very powerful `ForEach` methods. Folks have always pined for the lovely `ForEach` since the days of Borland Pascal's old `TCollection` object, and now it's back in full force, leveraging the power of anonymous methods. Thus, you can have a collection and very easily do what you please with the items.

Here is a simple example of just outputting them to the console window, but you can have your `TAction<T>` do anything at all that you like for each (sorry) element in the container.

[1]https://bitbucket.org/NickHodges/nickdemocode/

```
procedure SimpleForEachDemo;
var
  List: IList<integer>;
  Action: TAction<integer>;
  i: Integer;
begin
  Action := procedure(const aInt: integer) begin Writeln(Format('This number \
is: %d', [aInt])); end;

  List := TCollections.CreateList<integer>;
  for i := 1 to 10 do
  begin
    List.Add(Random(100));
  end;

  List.ForEach(Action);
end;
```

So, basically you have a lot of untapped power there in `Spring.Collections.pas`, eh? The use of `IEnumerable<T>` and predicates ought to transform your code and change the way you look for things in lists and collections. If you aren't using these powerful tools yet, I strongly recommend that you add them to your tool chest.

7.3 An Interview with `IEnumerable<T>` (IEoT):

Nick: Hey, IEoT, thanks for stopping by and chatting with us today

IEoT: No problem – I'm glad to do it.

Nick: First, let's talk about your role in Delphi. Up until now you haven't been very popular.

IEoT: Well, no, and that's bothered me. Delphi developers haven't really paid much attention to me as I think they believe that the Spring Framework is all about Dependency Injection. Don't get me wrong – I love `TContainer`. He's a great guy and fun to be around. But he's not all there is. I'm a powerful part of what Spring for Delphi does, and yeah, I won't lie – I've felt under-appreciated.

Nick: I can understand that.

IEoT: Well, I appreciate you having me on to talk about what I can do.

Nick: No worries, glad to do it. First up, tell me what this whole "of T" business is all about.

IEoT: Well, I can be a container for any type you like. Just define the type that you want me to keep track of, and I'll keep track of it for you. Any type at all. Doesn't matter.

Nick: So, you have been accused of being implemented too much. What do you have to say about that?

IEoT: Oh, you want to get into that, eh? Well, it's true that I get implemented by a lot of classes. But that just proves the power and usefulness of interfaces, right? I mean, who cares whether I'm a front for a list or a collection or whatever? That's sort of the point. I can do my thing no matter what is behind my scenes.

Nick: Well, sure, tell us a bit about what your basic methods do.

IEoT: Well, my most very basic functionality provides access to everything inside of the container I'm implementing. You can easily do a `for...in` on me and get out every item I contain. You can get my `First` item or my `Last`. You can get the biggest or the smallest with a simple method call. Shoot, you can even tell me how to compare two things together and I'll tell you the biggest of any complex type. But that's getting ahead of myself.

Nick: Yeah, let's hold off on that for now. Let's move on to some of the more advanced things you can do, say, with predicates.

IEoT: Yeah, predicates really let me strut my stuff. Pass me a predicate and you can really control what I return back. Predicates let you tell me what to keep and what to toss. Then I return all the keepers, and you have another instance of me with all of them in it. It's a win all around once you learn to use predicates. Want to keep all the strings that have more than three vowels in them? You can do it. And that's just if you pass me predicates.

Nick: What else can you be passed?

IEoT: Well, you can pass me actions. An action is just some code that I'll run against each element I have. I'll do anything you want to every item I have. Just call my `ForEach` method with an Action – probably it will be an Anonymous Method – and you have me do your will against everything I have. Pretty cool.

Nick: Indeed. What are some other things you can do?

IEoT: Well, let's see. I can be a list, a set, or an array if you want. I can tell you how many items I have, and I can tell you if I contain any given item. If I'm empty, I can let you know. Basically, I can tell you anything at all about the stuff I contain.

Nick: Hey, we are out of time. Thanks, `IEnumerable<T>`, for chatting with us.

IEoT: Thanks for having me.

8 Run-time Type Information

8.1 Introduction

Run-time Type Information (RTTI) is information about a class that the compiler gathers and attaches to a class at compile time. That information is then retrievable and modifiable by the developer at run-time – hence the name. At compile time, the compiler attaches information – metadata – about a given class to the class itself for retrieval and examination at runtime.

Delphi has had RTTI since Delphi 1.0. It is the old RTTI that lets the Object Inspector get and set property values in the Form Designer. However, the old RTTI system was not based on classes and was a bit cumbersome to use. The old RTTI system only stored information about published values.

Delphi 2010 introduced a very powerful new version of RTTI (found appropriately enough in the RTTI.pas unit) that provides run-time access to a class's fields, properties, and methods as well as the parameters of those methods.

In addition, the new RTTI means that you can attach your own runtime information to classes via attributes.

In this chapter, we look at basic RTTI, how you can find out almost anything about a given class at run-time. In the next chapter, we'll see how you can attach your own RTTI to a class with attributes, and end with a practical example of using RTTI.

Though it might seem complicated on the surface, RTTI is actually a rather simple feature. During the process of compiling, the compiler has a lot of information about the types that it is compiling. The compiler takes that information and "attaches" it to the class in the resulting binary. The RTTI unit contains a set of classes for retrieving this information from the binary. Unless you otherwise specify (and how to do that will be discussed below), RTTI is generated for every eligible type compiled into your binary, including classes, records, enumerated types, interfaces, ordinal types, and more.

With RTTI, you can do the following:

- Gather information about the fields, properties, and methods of a type, including the parameters of those methods.
- Get and set values for fields and properties
- Invoke any method, including passing values for any number of parameters, and returning values for functions.

However, before you can really dive into RTTI, you need to understand one of its basic building blocks, TValue.

8.2 TValue

TValue is a new record type that was introduced along with the new RTTI in Delphi 2010. In some ways it is similar to a variant, but it is not the same, and should not be used as such. It is able to hold data of various types, and it can convert that data to types that are assignment compatible, such as Integer to Word or Char to String. It wasn't designed to be used as a variant – where you could change its type easily – but instead as a transport for getting data from its concrete values to dynamic RTTI and back. A TValue can't change its type once set.

TValue can hold virtually any Delphi type. Its declaration includes a private field FValueData of type TValueData which is declared as follows:

```
TValueData = record
FTypeInfo: PTypeInfo;
// FValueData vs old FHeapData:
// FHeapData doubled as storage for interfaces. However, that was ambiguous
// in the case of nil interface values: FTypeInfo couldn't be trusted
// because it looked like the structure was uninitialized. Then, DataSize
// would be 0.
// FValueData is different: interfaces are always stored like strings etc.,
// as a reference stored in a blob on the heap.
FValueData: IValueData;
case Integer of
  0: (FAsUByte: Byte);
  1: (FAsUWord: Word);
  2: (FAsULong: LongWord);
  3: (FAsObject: Pointer);
  4: (FAsClass: TClass);
  5: (FAsSByte: Shortint);
  6: (FAsSWord: Smallint);
  7: (FAsSLong: Longint);
  8: (FAsSingle: Single);
  9: (FAsDouble: Double);
  10: (FAsExtended: Extended);
  11: (FAsComp: Comp);
  12: (FAsCurr: Currency);
  13: (FAsUInt64: UInt64);
  14: (FAsSInt64: Int64);
  15: (FAsMethod: TMethod);
  16: (FAsPointer: Pointer);
end;
```

Thus, it is capable of being type compatible with any of the data types listed above, including any

Delphi object. However, the one thing that they cannot do is change their established type or be assigned to a different type. Thus, the following code will not compile:

```
var
  V: TValue;
  i: integer;
begin
  V := 42;
  i := V; // You can't do this
end;
```

However, the following code will compile, as TValue can be asked to cast itself into a compatible type:

```
var
  V: TValue;
  i: integer;
begin
  V := 42;
  i := V.AsInteger; // You can do this
end;
```

Once set to an integer, though, it cannot be cast as a string:

```
// This will not compile
// i := v;
// but this will
i := v.AsInteger;
// and this will not
//s := V.AsString;
```

These simple demos should serve to show that TValue is designed to accept arbitrary types, transport them, and then easily get their original type back. They aren't really designed to accept one type and become another.

TValue does have the smarts to cast itself to another TValue with a compatible type, however:

```
var
  V: TValue;
begin
  V := 42;
  V2 := V.Cast<Byte>;
  WriteLn('V2 is now a Byte: ', V2.ToString);
end;
```

And you can use the IsType<T> method to prove it:

```
if V.IsType<Byte> then
begin
  WriteLn('Yes it is true, V is a Byte');
end else
begin
  WriteLn('Oops, V is not a Byte');
end;
```

In addition to holding the standard types, TValue allows you to declare your own types and the "make" them into a TValue. For instance, given this record type...

```
type
TExampleRecord = record
  SomeInt: integer;
  SomeBytes: array[0..5] of Char;
end;
```

...you can put data into an instance:

```
  var
    ERIn: TExampleRecord;

  ...

  ERIn.SomeInt := 99;
  ERIn.SomeBytes[0] := 'a';
  ERIn.SomeBytes[1] := 'b';
  ERIn.SomeBytes[2] := 'c';
  ERIn.SomeBytes[3] := 'd';
  ERIn.SomeBytes[4] := 'e';
  ERIn.SomeBytes[5] := 'f';
```

And once you have that record, you can call the TValue.Make method to create an instance of TValue that holds a TExampleRecord.

```
    // We can create our very own type and make it a TValue
    TValue.Make(@ERIn, TypeInfo(TExampleRecord), V2);
```

In this example, V2 becomes the TValue that holds TExampleRecord, and so we can report out on it using the following code:

```
if V2.IsType<TExampleRecord> then
begin
  WriteLn('V2 is a TExampleRecord');
end else
begin
  WriteLn('V2 is NOT a TExampleRecord');
end;


EROut := V2.AsType<TExampleRecord>;


WriteLn('EROut.SomeInt = ', EROut.SomeInt);
Write('And this ought to be the first six letters in the alphabet: ');
for C in EROut.SomeBytes do
begin
  Write(C);
end;
WriteLn;
```

The above shows that once you Make your TValue with your own type, you can still extract the information that was put into it.

Thus TValue can hold any type needed as part of the larger RTTI eco-system.

8.3 RTTI on Classes

The basic functionality of RTTI is to look at the features of a class. So let's define a class that we can then use RTTI to look at:

```
unit uRTTIDemoClass;

interface

type
  TRTTIDemoClass = class
  private
    FPrivateField: integer;
    FPublicProperty: string;
    FIndexedProperty: array of string;
    procedure PrivateMethod;
    procedure SetPublicProperty(const Value: string);
    function GetIndexedProperty(aIndex: integer): string;
    procedure SetIndexedProperty(aIndex: integer; const Value: string);
  protected
    procedure ProtectedMethod;
  public
    PublicField: Double;
    procedure PublicMethod;
    procedure PublicMethodWithParams(aString: string; aExtended: Extended);
    property PublicProperty: string read FPublicProperty write SetPublicProperty;
    property IndexedProperty[aIndex: integer]: string read GetIndexedProperty wri\
te SetIndexedProperty;
  end;

implementation

function TRTTIDemoClass.GetIndexedProperty(aIndex: integer): string;
begin
  Result := FIndexedProperty[aIndex];
end;

procedure TRTTIDemoClass.PrivateMethod;
begin
  WriteLn('This is a private method');
end;

procedure TRTTIDemoClass.ProtectedMethod;
begin
  WriteLn('This is a protected method');
end;
```

```
procedure TRTTIDemoClass.PublicMethod;
begin
  WriteLn('This is a public method');
end;

procedure TRTTIDemoClass.PublicMethodWithParams(aString: string; aExtended: Exten\
ded);
begin
  WriteLn('You passed in ', aString, ' and ', aExtended);
end;

procedure TRTTIDemoClass.SetIndexedProperty(aIndex: integer; const Value: string);
begin
  FIndexedProperty[aIndex] := Value;
end;

procedure TRTTIDemoClass.SetPublicProperty(const Value: string);
begin
  FPublicProperty := Value;
end;

end.
```

TRTTIDemoClass contains all the various fields, methods, and properties that can be detected by RTTI. Thus, it is illustrative of what RTTI can do.

Delphi's RTTI all starts with the TRttiContext record. It is the record from which all RTTI information flows. The basic function of TRttiContext is to find and return an TRttiType instance for a given type that will be examined. So for our demo, the first line of code will be:

```
var
  Context: TRTTIContext;
  TempType: TRttiType;
begin
  TempType := Context.GetType(TRTTIDemoClass.ClassInfo);
  ...
end;
```

In the above code, Context is used to get the type information for our demo class and return it as a TRttiType. TRttiContext provides access to all RTTI information for the whole binary and thus is the main access point to that information. TRttiContext can retrieve RTTI for a specific type via its TClass information. It can get an array containing RTTI for every type in the binary, or it can get the information for a specific type based on its fully qualified name.

TRttiType

TRttiType holds the information about a given type. Given the above code, TempType is now a reference to the RTTI for TRTTIDemoClass. Below is part of the public interface that contains the most common methods for accessing the information about the given type:

```
function GetMethods: TArray<TRttiMethod>; overload; virtual;
function GetFields: TArray<TRttiField>; virtual;
function GetProperties: TArray<TRttiProperty>; virtual;
function GetIndexedProperties: TArray<TRttiIndexedProperty>; virtual;

function GetMethod(const AName: string): TRttiMethod; virtual;
function GetMethods(const AName: string): TArray<TRttiMethod>; overload; virtual;
function GetField(const AName: string): TRttiField; virtual;
function GetProperty(const AName: string): TRttiProperty; virtual;
function GetIndexedProperty(const AName: string): TRttiIndexedProperty; virtual;
```

> Note the RTTI for indexed properties (the last function above) only is available in XE2 and above.

TRttiType is the class that actually holds all the RTTI information about the class being inspected. Using the methods listed above, you can ask it for all the fields, properties, and methods of the given class. You can ask for all in an array, or a specific item by name.

To get a TRttiType, you call TRttiContext.GetType(), an overloaded method. You can pass it a TClass reference or a pointer to the type information for a given class. Above, we've gotten the TempType reference with a call to the ClassInfo class method of TRTTIDemoClass.

Each member type has a specific RTTI type assigned to it. Fields have a TRttiField class to describe them. There is also TRttiMethod, TRttiProperty, and TRttiIndexedProperty. Each TRttiMethod has within it the TRttiParameter classes needed to define the parameters (if any) associated with the method.

TRttiField

RTTI is available for all fields of a class regardless of scope. So, for instance, you can call:

```
TempType := Context.GetType(TRTTIDemoClass);
// Fields
WriteLn(TempType.Name, ' has the following fields: ');
for TempField in TempType.GetFields do
begin
  WriteLn('  ', TempField.ToString, ' with visiblility: '
          , GetEnumName(TypeInfo(TMemberVisibility)
          , Integer(TempField.Visibility)));
end;
```

and that will output to the console all the field names of the given class including the visibility of the field. The call to GetFields returns a TArray<TRttiFields>, which you can then enumerate over.

If you have the name of a field as a string, you can call:

```
TempField := TempType.GetField('FPrivateField');
```

and gain access that way.

TRttiField encapsulates all the information about the field. You've seen the Name and Visibility fields above. In addition, the ToString method will return the fields name, type, and hex offset from the memory location allocated for the class.

TRttiProperty

Properties work basically the same as fields. TRttiType has GetProperties and GetMethods methods that return arrays of the appropriate type. It also has GetProperty which takes a string value of the exact name of the item being asked for.

The following code will print out the properties of our demo class:

```
WriteLn(TempType.Name, ' has the following properties:');
for TempProperty in TempType.GetProperties do
begin
  WriteLn('  ', TempProperty.ToString, ' with the visibility: ', GetEnumName(Type\
Info(TMemberVisibility), Integer(TempProperty.Visibility)));
end;
```

Likewise, you can gather information about the indexed properties of a class:

```
WriteLn(TempType.Name, ' has the following indexed properties:');
for TempIdxProperty in TempType.GetIndexedProperties do
begin
  WriteLn('  ', TempIdxProperty.ToString, ' with the visibility: '
          , GetEnumName(TypeInfo(TMemberVisibility)
          , Integer(TempIdxProperty.Visibility)));
end;
```

TRttiMethod

Methods can be extracted in much the same way. However, methods also provide information about their parameters. The `TRttiMethod` class can enumerate its parameters like so:

```
// Methods
WriteLn(TempType.Name, ' has the following methods:');
for TempMethod in TempType.GetDeclaredMethods do
begin
  WriteLn('  ', TempMethod.Name);
  TempParams := TempMethod.GetParameters;
  if Length(TempParams) > 0 then
  begin
    for TempParam in TempParams do
    begin
      WriteLn('    ', TempParam.ToString);
    end;
  end else
  begin
    WriteLn('    ', 'No Parameters');
  end;
end;
```

This code checks to see if the method in question is a method directly on `TRTTIDemoClass` by using the `GetDeclaredMethods` instead of just `GetMethods`, which returns all methods, including those from parent classes. If the method has any parameters, those are listed as well.

8.4 Using RTTI to Affect Instances

The previous examples all worked on classes, as opposed to instances. In other words, the RTTI retrieved information from a `TClass` reference as opposed to an instance of that `TClass`. However, Delphi's RTTI library allows you to retrieve information from live instances. It also allows you to set values and execute methods on those instances. Pretty cool, eh?

So let's take a look. Again, we'll be using our demo class, `TRTTIDemoClass` to show how things work.

Getting and Setting Values

One of the basic things to do with a class instance is to set and retrieve values of variables. Delphi's RTTI lets you do that for any field of a class.

The first thing to note is that you must have a valid instance of a class that you want to alter. Once you have that, RTTI will take it as a parameter and operate on it as desired. For instance, here is some code that will take an instance of TRTTIDemoClass and set values for its field called 'FPrivateField:

Note that the type of the parameter sent to the SetValue field that sets the new value is our old pal TValue. The code illustrates this by setting the new value to a TValue explicitly:

```
WriteLn('Getting and setting a private field....');
TempType := Context.GetType(TRTTIDemoClass.ClassInfo);
TempField := TempType.GetField('FPrivateField');
NewValue := 'This is a new value for PublicProperty held by a TValue';
TempField.SetValue(RDC, NewValue);
WriteLn('You can get the value using RTTI: ', TempField.GetValue(RDC).ToString);
```

Note that you can't get at the value you've set from the object itself, but you can access it via RTTI.

And as a side note, while RTTI allows you to do it, it is bad practice to change the values of internal fields on a class. Instead, you should use the properties of a class to alter its internal state.

Properties work almost exactly the same way, except we can "prove" that the value was set by asking for the value directly from the instance:

```
WriteLn('Getting and setting a property...');
TempProperty := TempType.GetProperty('PublicProperty');
NewValue := 'NewValue for PublicProperty';
TempProperty.SetValue(RDC, NewValue);
WriteLn('PublicProperty is now set to: ', RDC.PublicProperty);
WriteLn('You can also get the value using RTTI: ', TempProperty.GetValue(RDC).ToS\
tring);
```

Indexed properties work exactly as you'd expect:

```
TempIdxProperty := TempType.GetIndexedProperty('IndexedProperty');
NewValue := 'This is index 0';
TempIdxProperty.SetValue(RDC, [0], NewValue);
NewValue := 'This is index 1';
TempIdxProperty.SetValue(RDC, [1], NewValue);
WriteLn('IndexedProperty[0] retrieved via RTTI: ', TempIdxProperty.GetValue(RDC, \
[0]).ToString);
WriteLn('IndexedProperty[1] retrieved right from the instance: ', RDC.IndexedProp\
erty[1]);
```

Thus, any field or property can be set or retrieved using Delphi's RTTI library. But wait, there's more! – you can actually invoke any public method.

Invoking Methods

Not only can you set and get values of a class instance, you can also call its methods. The TRttiMethod class has a method called Invoke that takes two parameters:

```
function TRttiMethod.Invoke(Instance: TObject; const Args: array of TValue): TVal\
ue;
```

The first is the instance itself whose method you are going to call. The second is an array of TValue that represent the parameters that are passed to the method. If the method is a function, then the result of that function call is returned as a TValue by the call to Invoke.

```
procedure CallMethodsWithRTTI;
var
  RDC: TRTTIDemoClass;
  Context: TRttiContext;
  TempType: TRttiType;
  TempMethod: TRttiMethod;
  TempParameters: TArray<TRttiParameter>;
  TempParameter: TRttiParameter;
  TempValue: TValue;
  TempResult: TValue;
  ParameterValues: array[0..1] of TValue;
  i: Integer;
begin
  RDC := TRTTIDemoClass.Create;
  try
    TempType := Context.GetType(TRTTIDemoClass);
```

```
for TempMethod in TempType.GetDeclaredMethods do
begin
  // Ignore constructor and grab only public methods
  if (TempMethod.Visibility <>  mvPublic) then Continue;
  if TempMethod.IsConstructor then Continue;
  WriteLn('About to invoke the method named: ', TempMethod.Name);
  case TempMethod.MethodKind of
    mkProcedure: begin
                   TempParameters := TempMethod.GetParameters;
                   // We know the possibilities here...
                   i := 0;

                   case Length(TempParameters) of
                     0: TempMethod.Invoke(RDC, []);
                     1: TempMethod.Invoke(RDC, [0]);
                     2: begin
                          for TempParameter in TempParameters do
                          begin
                            case TempParameter.ParamType.TypeKind of
                              tkString,
                              tkUString: TempValue := 'Passed in via Invoke';
                              tkFloat:   TempValue := 3.14159;
                              tkInteger: TempValue := 0;
                            end;
                            ParameterValues[i] := TempValue;
                            inc(i);
                          end;

                          TempMethod.Invoke(RDC, [ParameterValues[0], Parame\
terValues[1]]);
                        end;
                   end;
                 end;
    mkFunction:  begin
                   // Ignore the property getters
                   if not UpperCase(TempMethod.Name).Contains('GET') then
                   begin
                     TempResult := TempMethod.Invoke(RDC, []);
                     WriteLn('Result of a call to ', TempMethod.Name, ': ', \
TempResult.ToString);
                   end;
                 end;
```

```
      else
        Continue;
      end;
    end;
  finally
    RDC.Free;
  end;
end;
```

The above code does the following things:

- It creates an instance of TRTTIDemoClass so that an active instance can be called. It may not be totally obvious – but you need to have a live instance to call.
- It gets a TRttiType for TRTTIDemo class. Then, it enumerates over each of the methods for that type.
- It enumerates only the declared – that is, declared in TRTTIDemoClass itself – and ignores the constructor and any non-public method.
- Then it checks the MethodType property to see if it is a procedure or a function.

  - If it is a procedure, it determines the parameters and calls Invoke on the method. We've cheated a little bit here, as the code knows exactly that the parameters are and acts accordingly.
  - If it is a function, it calls the function, captures the result, and displays it.

8.5 General Notes

Some additional things to note about Delphi's RTTI:

- You can use the IsClassMethod and the IsStatic calls to determine, well, if the method is a class method or if it is a static method.
- If the method is a class method, you can call it by passing the ClassType to Invoke as the first parameter without having a valid instance.
- You can also retrieve the calling convention and the dispatch type of a method, as well as a pointer to its actual location in the Virtual Method Table.

8.6 RTTI for Non-classes

Classes are probably the most common use case, but Delphi can also track RTTI for non-class types such as records, enumerations, ordinal types, and others.

RTTI for Ordinal Types

You can gather RTTI about the various ordinal types. Consider the following code:

```
var
  Context: TRttiContext;
  TempType: TRttiType;
  TempOrd: TRTTIOrdinalType;
  TempName: string;
begin
  // Ordinal
  TempType := Context.GetType(TypeInfo(Byte));
  if TempType.IsOrdinal then
  begin
    TempOrd := TempType as TRTTIOrdinalType;
    WriteLn('The minimum value for ', TempOrd.Name, ' is: ', TempOrd.MinValue);
    WriteLn('The maximum value for ', TempOrd.Name, ' is: ', TempOrd.MaxValue);
  end;
end;
```

Here we grab the RTTI for a Byte, and display the minimum (0) and maximum (255) available values.

RTTI for Records

Records can have RTTI attached to them as well. Their RTTI works very similarly to that of a class:

```
  // Record
  TempType := Context.GetType(TypeInfo(TDemoRecord));
  if TempType.IsRecord then
  begin
    TempRecord := TempType.AsRecord;
    WriteLn(TempRecord.Name, ' has the following methods: ');
    for TempMethod in TempRecord.GetMethods do
    begin
      WriteLn('  ', TempMethod.Name);
    end;
    WriteLn('... and the following fields:');
    for TempField in TempRecord.GetFields do
    begin
      WriteLn('  ', TempField.Name);
    end;
    WriteLn;
  end;
```

RTTI for Arrays

You can determine general information about arrays as well:

```
// Arrays
TempType := Context.GetType(TypeInfo(TThreeStringArray));
if TempType.TypeKind = tkArray then
begin
  TempArrayType := TempType as TRttiArrayType;
  WriteLn(TempArrayType.Name, ' is a ', TempArrayType.DimensionCount, ' dimensi\
on array with a total of ', TempArrayType.TotalElementCount, ' elements of type '\
, TempArrayType.ElementType.Name);
end;
```

8.7 Miscellaneous Methods

There are a few other things that you can do with Delphi's RTTI:

- Every RTTI object has a `Parent` property that tells you its owning member. So for instance, a parameter is parented by a method, which in turn is parented by a type.
- The `TRttiType` class can tell you if a type `IsManaged` (strings and interfaces), `IsOrdinal`, `IsRecord`, and
- `TRttiType` has a set of methods that find the "Declared" fields, properties, and methods. The methods with "Declared" in their names return only those items actually declared in the class itself and not its ancestors.
- RTTI is also available for interfaces via the `TRttiInterfaceType` class. You can grab the GUID and declared methods for any interface.

8.8 RTTI Compiler Directives

The new RTTI features are cool and powerful, but one of the downsides is that it adds a lot of data to the resulting binary. In order to limit that increase in size, Delphi provides a set of compiler directives that can be used to limit the amount of RTTI information that is stored.

> I should add that this section covers code that should fall into the "*only do this if you really know what you are doing*" area. Turning off RTTI, even for certain portions of your code, could make your code stop working as expected, especially if you are using libraries that expect RTTI to be present, like an object-relational mapping library, a Dependency Injection container, etc.

If you want to turn off RTTI for all the units in your application, then put this at the top of your DPR file, right before the uses clause:

```
{$WEAKLINKRTTI ON}
{$RTTI EXPLICIT METHODS([]) PROPERTIES([]) FIELDS([])}
```

This will tell the compiler to not put RTTI into any of your code. Note that it will not prevent RTTI from being compiled into the VCL, FMX, or any third-party code.

This same code can be placed in individual units if you want to limit the RTTI for only the classes in that unit. Placing it in the DPR makes the directives valid application wide. You should place these directives only when you aren't going to be using RTTI within the scope of the directives.

The {$WEAKLINKRTTI ON} directive tells the compiler to not place RTTI on methods of classes that are not directly referenced. By default, the compiler includes RTTI for all methods of classes, whether they are called directly or not. This is done to ensure that any class method can be invoked dynamically if desired. If you know that a given class or unit will not be invoked dynamically, you can use the {$WEAKLINKRTTI} directive to tell the compiler not to include the RTTI for methods not directly referenced in code.

However, if a class is declared but never instantiated, then no RTTI will be generated for it and the class will not be present anywhere in the resulting binary.

Note that the {$WEAKLINKRTTI} directive only affects linking and not compiling. That is, it doesn't affect the information placed into DCU files, but only the information linked from them.

The {$RTTI} directive gives you more control over exactly what RTTI information is and isn't emitted by the compiler for classes within the scope of the directive.

The first parameter will be one of two values: INHERIT or EXPLICIT. INHERIT indicates that the RTTI directives will be inherited from its base class. That is, if you have

```
{$RTTI INHERIT}
TChild = class(TParent)
```

then TChild will contain inherit the {$RTTI} directives from TParent.

EXPLICIT will do the opposite. If you declare:

```
{$RTTI EXPLICIT}
TChild = class(TParent)
```

then TChild will not contain the RTTI directives for TParent, but only for its own declared methods, properties, and fields. The EXPLICIT parameter will remove all previous {$RTTI} directives from parent classes and assert the directives directly on the class.

You can even have more fine control over the emitted RTTI than that. You can use the METHODS, PROPERTIES and FIELDS parameters to limit specifically the RTTI for those members. Furthermore, you can declare for each whether the scope included should be vcPrivate, vcProtected, vcPublic, and/or vcPublished.

For instance, if you wanted to declare a class and have only the public properties and fields as well as the public and published methods included with RTTI, you could declare the following directive:

```
{$RTTI EXPLICIT PROPERTIES([vcPublic]) FIELDS([vcPublic]) METHODS([vcPublic vcPub\
lished])}
```

In this way, you can fine tune your classes to emit exactly the amount and scope of RTTI that you want.

One thing to note is that if you have published members, the compiler will automatically turn on the {$METHODINFO ON} switch, meaning that the published fields will have RTTI information included for them, and there doesn't seem to be any way to convince the compiler not to do that – not even with explicitly turning off MethodInfo with the {$M-} switch.

Thus, given the following class:

```
type
  {$M-}
  {$RTTI EXPLICIT METHODS([vcPublic]) PROPERTIES([vcPublic]) FIELDS([vcPublic])}
  TPublicStuffOnly = class(TObject)
  private
    PrivateField: double;
    FPublicPropertyField: string;
    FPublishedPropertyField: string;
    procedure PrivateMethod;
  protected
    ProtectedField: string;
    procedure ProtectedMethod;
  public
    PublicField: integer;
    procedure PublicMethod;
    property PublicProperty: string read FPublicPropertyField write FPublicProper\
tyField;
  published
    {$M-}
    PublishedField: TObject;
    function PublishedMethod(aParam: string): integer;
    property PublishedProperty: string read FPublishedPropertyField write FPublis\
hedPropertyField;
    {$M+}
  end;
```

This code will output only the public and published fields, properties and methods of TPublicStuffOnly.

```
procedure DisplayLimitedRTTI;
var
  Context: TRttiContext;
  TempType: TRttiType;
  TempMethod: TRttiMethod;
  TempProperty: TRttiProperty;
  TempField: TRttiField;
begin
  WriteLn('There should only be public fields listed below for ', TPublicStuffOnl\
y.ClassName);
  TempType := Context.GetType(TPublicStuffOnly);
  WriteLn('Fields:');
  for TempField in TempType.GetDeclaredFields do
  begin
    WriteLn('  ', TempField.Name);
  end;

  WriteLn('Properties:');
  for TempProperty in TempType.GetDeclaredProperties do
  begin
    WriteLn('  ', TempProperty.Name);
  end;

  WriteLn('Methods:');
  for TempMethod in TempType.GetDeclaredMethods do
  begin
    WriteLn('  ', TempMethod.Name);
  end;
end;
```

Strong Type Linking

If you create a class, put in in your app, but never actually instantiate it, then by default, that class will not be included in the resulting binary, and since the class isn't there, there naturally won't be any resulting RTTI for the class. If you want to ensure that *every* class is included and that all those classes include RTTI, you can use the following compiler directive:

```
{$STRONGLINKTYPES ON}
```

If you want it to be effective for the entire binary, then you need to include it in the DPR file. Note that this directive is not required for a Delphi package (BPL) because a package includes all classes and RTTI by default.

8.9 Conclusion

So there you have the basics of Run-time Type Information. In this chapter, we saw how you can identify, evaluate, set, and invoke the fields, properties, and methods of classes and records. In the next chapter we'll see how you can add your own custom run-time information to classes via a feature called Attributes.

9 Attributes

9.1 Introduction

Okay, so far we've seen how Delphi's compiler attaches RTTI meta-data to your classes and other types. We've seen how you can control the extent of RTTI which is included in your binary. And so here is this chapter's rhetorical question: Wouldn't it be cool if you could attach your own custom information to a class, method, property, field, or parameter?

Why yes, it would be cool! And as always, I would never ask this question if the answer weren't "Yes, you can do that!". So, yes, you can do that through a language feature called attributes. By adding attributes to classes, records and other items, you can define your own run-time information that can then be retrieved using the RTTI framework.

9.2 What are Attributes

Attributes are very simple. You can declare a custom attribute as a descendant of TCustomAttribute, a class declared in System.pas.

```
// Defines a simple attribute
SimpleAttribute = class(TCustomAttribute)
private
  FNumber: integer;
public
  constructor Create(aNumber: integer);
  property Number: integer read FNumber;
end;
```

That's all there is to a basic attribute – it's a simple class that declares an integer property. Things get even simpler when you see that TCustomAttribute itself is a direct descendant of TObject:

```
TCustomAttribute = class(TObject)
end;
```

That's it – seriously. An attribute is nothing more than a class that descends from TCustomAttribute and which can, if desired, have properties and a constructor to set the properties. The constructor is needed because you can pass parameters to it in the attribute declaration.

As a general rule, a custom attribute will have a property for each item passed to the constructor. The constructor will keep the values passed to it as read-only properties. Those property values will then be available at run-time for your retrieval.

So how do you add an attribute to the RTTI for your binary? Attributes are declared with square brackets:

```
TAttributeOnProperty = class
private
  function GetBottlesOfBeer: string;
public
  [SimpleAttribute(99)] // Attribute on a property
  property BottlesOfBeer: string read GetBottlesOfBeer;
end;
```

Note a couple of things:

- The attribute declaration is surrounded by square brackets.
- The attribute takes a single integer, which corresponds to the single integer parameter in the constructor. There is no need to explicitly call Create, and if you do, the compiler will complain.
- By convention, the phrase 'Attribute' is actually optional – the attribute can be declared as [Simple(99)] which the compiler treats exactly the same as [SimpleAttribute(99)]
- Also by convention, attributes don't start with the traditional T.
- Attributes can be placed almost anywhere in a class: on the class itself, as well as on fields, properties, methods, and even on the parameters of methods.
- Attributes can have methods that you can also call at run-time if so desired.

When an attribute is attached to a class member, the compiler will take the information from the declaration and attach it to the item just like regular RTTI information.

And then, getting the custom attribute information is done as follows:

```
function TAttributeOnProperty.GetPropertyAttribute: string;
var
  Context: TRttiContext;
  TempType: TRttiType;
  TempProperty: TRttiProperty;
  TempAttributes: TArray<TCustomAttribute>;
  TempValue: TValue;
  Attribute: TCustomAttribute;
begin
```

```
  Result := '';
  TempType := Context.GetType(Self.ClassType);
  TempProperty := TempType.GetProperty('BottlesOfBeer');
  TempAttributes := TempProperty.GetAttributes;
  for Attribute in TempAttributes do
  begin
    if Attribute is SimpleAttribute then
    begin
      TempValue := SimpleAttribute(Attribute).Number;
    end;
  end;
  Result := TempValue.ToString;
end;
```

This routine grabs the value of the Number property on an attached attribute and returns it as a string. It does that by:

- First, grabbing the type information for the class that has a property that has SimpleAttribute attached to it.
- Next, it finds that property using GetProperty. In this case, the property is named 'BottlesOf-Beer'.
- Once it has a reference to the property, it calls GetAttributes to get an array of all the attributes for that property. Note any element can have any number of attributes declared on it. Note, as well, that the call to GetAttributes returns an array of TCustomAttribute, which will be the very class (or classes) that is declared as the attribute.
- Then, the code enumerates over all the attributes determining if any of them are of type SimpleAttribute. If so, then we know that the Attribute variable is in fact an instance of SimpleAttribute, and thus we can cast it polymorphically and call anything we want on it, including determining its properties and calling its methods.

As mentioned above, attributes can be placed in numerous types of places on a class. Consider the following code, which demonstrates all the places that attributes might be placed.

```
type
  SampleAttribute = class(TCustomAttribute);


[Sample]
TAttributesEverywhere = class
private
  [Sample]
  FSomeProperty: Extended;
  procedure SetSomeProperty(const Value: Extended);
public
[Sample]
  procedure DoThis([Sample]aString: string);
  [Sample]
function DoThat([Sample]aObject: TObject): integer;
  [Sample]
  property SomeProperty: Extended read FSomeProperty write SetSomeProperty;
end;
```

Here we see the Sample attribute being placed at numerous locations. The following code hunts them all up and displays them in the console window:

```
procedure DoAttributesEverywhere;
var
  Context: TRTTIContext;
  TempClassType: TRttiType;
  TempEnumType: TRttiOrdinalType;
  TempAttribute: TCustomAttribute;
  TempAttribute1: TCustomAttribute;
  TempField: TRttiField;
  TempMethod: TRttiMethod;
  TempParam: TRttiParameter;
  TempProperty: TRttiProperty;
begin
  // Enum
  TempEnumType := Context.GetType(TypeInfo(TStopLight)).AsOrdinal;
  for TempAttribute in TempEnumType.GetAttributes do
  begin
    WriteLn(TempEnumType.Name, ' has the following attributes: ');
    Write('  ', TempAttribute.ToString);
  end;
  WriteLn;
  WriteLn;
```

```
// Class
TempClassType := Context.GetType(TAttributesEverywhere);
WriteLn('TAttributesEverywhere has the following attributes:');

for TempAttribute in TempClassType.GetAttributes do
begin
  WriteLn('  Class Attribute: ', TempAttribute.ToString);
end;
WriteLn;
// Fields
for TempField in TempClassType.GetFields do
begin
  WriteLn('The ', TempField.Name, ' has the following attributes:');
  for TempAttribute in TempField.GetAttributes do
  begin
    WriteLn(' ', TempAttribute.ToString);
  end;
end;
WriteLn;
// Methods
for TempMethod in TempClassType.GetMethods do
begin
  for TempAttribute in TempMethod.GetAttributes do
  begin
    WriteLn('The ', TempMethod.Name, 'method has the ', TempAttribute.T\
oString, ' attribute.');
    for TempParam in TempMethod.GetParameters do
    begin
      for TempAttribute1 in TempParam.GetAttributes do
      begin
        WriteLn('  The ', TempParam.Name, ' parameter has the ', TempAt\
tribute1.ToString, ' attribute.');
      end;
      if TempMethod.ReturnType <> nil then
      begin
        Writeln('  The ', TempMethod.Name, ' method is a function that \
returns a ', TempMethod.ReturnType.Name, '.');
      end else
      begin
        WriteLn('  The ', TempMethod.Name, ' method is a procedure.');
      end;
```

```
              end;
            end;
          end;
        WriteLn;
        // Properties
        for TempProperty in TempClassType.GetProperties do
        begin
          for TempAttribute in TempProperty.GetAttributes do
          begin
            WriteLn('The ', TempProperty.Name, ' has the ', TempAttribute.ToStr\
ing, ' property.');
          end;
        end;
      end;
```

As noted, a given item can have multiple attributes attached to it:

```
    type
      FirstAttribute = class(TCustomAttribute);

      SecondAttribute = class(TCustomAttribute);

      ThirdAttribute = class(TCustomAttribute);

      [First][Second][Third]
      TMultipleAttributes = class(TObject);
```

Each of those attributes can be retrieved as well:

```
        procedure DoMultipleAttributes;
        var
          Context: TRTTIContext;
          TempType: TRttiType;
          TempAttribute: TCustomAttribute;
        begin
          TempType := Context.GetType(TMultipleAttributes);
          WriteLn(TMultipleAttributes.ClassName, ' has the following attributes: \
');
          for TempAttribute in TempType.GetAttributes do
          begin
            WriteLn('  ', TempAttribute.ToString);
          end;
        end;
```

Here are some important things to note about attributes in general:

- They are retrieved basically the same way that fields, methods, and properties are retrieved. One difference is that you can only retrieve all the attributes via a call to GetAttributes. There is no way to get a single attribute by name as there is with methods, properties, and fields.
- Another subtle difference is that the call to GetAttributes will return an array of the actual attributes themselves and not a class that is part of the RTTI unit. This means that once you have a reference to the attribute, you can treat it like a regular class. This also means that you can add fields, properties, and methods to the class that are available at runtime.

If you declare an unknown attribute anywhere in your code, the compiler will accept it, but you will receive the following compiler warning: W1025 Unsupported language feature: 'custom attribute'

9.3 A Simple Example

Attributes can be very useful. They are most often used to tag items in your code with useful information. For example, you may have a class that you want to display as part of your UI. However, when you do, you don't want the identifier names in your code to be used to display the labels for the associated data. Instead, you can 'tag' the properties that you want to display with an attribute. First, you can declare an attribute type that will take as a single string parameter the text that you want to use in the label:

```
type

  DisplayTextAttribute = class(TCustomAttribute)
  private
    FDisplayText: string;
  public
    constructor Create(aDisplayText: string);
    property DisplayText: string read FDisplayText write FDisplayText;
  end;
```

Then, you place that attribute on each of the properties that you want to display:

```
type
  TCustomer = Class(TObject)
  private
    FFirstName: string;
    FLastName: string;
    FStreetAddress: string;
    FZIP: string;
    FState: string;
    FCity: string;
  ` FPhone: string;
  public
    [DisplayText('First Name')]
    property FirstName: string read FFirstName write FFirstName;
    [DisplayText('Last Name')]
    property LastName: string read FLastName write FLastName;
    [DisplayText('Street Address')]
    property StreetAddress: string read FStreetAddress write FStreetAddress;
    [DisplayText('City')]
    property City: string read FCity write FCity;
    [DisplayText('State')]
    property State: string read FState write FState;
    [DisplayText('ZIP Code')]
    property ZIP: string read FZIP write FZIP;
    [DisplayText('Phone #')]
    property Phone: string read FPhone write FPhone;
  end;
```

Once the labels are defined for each property, you can retrieve them. In the code below, we grab the property name and the display text and put them into a name/value pair within a TStringList for easy retrieval:

```
procedure GetAllDisplayTextsForClass(aType: TClass; const aStringList: TStrings);

  function GetDisplayTextForProperty(aProp: TRTTIProperty; aPropName: string): \
string;
  var
    TempAttribute: TCustomAttribute;
  begin
    Result := '';
    if aProp <> nil then
    begin
      for TempAttribute in aProp.GetAttributes do
```

```
      begin
        if TempAttribute is TDisplayTextAttribute then
        begin
          Result := TDisplayTextAttribute(TempAttribute).DisplayText;
        end;
      end;
    end;
  end;

var
  TempContext: TRttiContext;
  TempProp: TRTTIProperty;
  TempType: TRttiType;
  TempName, TempValue: string;
begin
  if aStringList = nil then
    Exit;
  aStringList.Clear;
  TempContext := TRttiContext.Create;
  try
    TempType := TempContext.GetType(aType);
    for TempProp in TempType.GetProperties do
    begin
      TempName := TempProp.Name;
      TempValue := GetDisplayTextForProperty(TempProp, TempName);
      aStringList.Values[TempName] := TempValue;
    end;
  finally
    TempContext.Free;
  end;
end;
```

9.4 Conclusion

Attributes are cool. You can use them to add specific data to the RTTI of your classes, records, and enumerations. You can easily retrieve that data and use it in your applications, enabling your code to be richer and more complete with the addition of some simple syntax. If you aren't using attributes to decorate your code, you should start.

9.5 An Interview with Attributes

Nick: Attributes, thanks for sitting down with me today. Very much appreciated

Attribute: Glad to do it – I like to help out where I can.

Nick: Speaking of that, where can you help out?

Attribute: I can pretty much help out anywhere. I'm happy to tag along on enumerations, classes, methods, parameters, properties – almost anywhere.

Nick: And what do you like to do when you tag along?

Attribute: Well, I can mark things. For instance, if you want a method to be a test in a testing framework, you might add me like this: `[Test]`.

Nick: And you can actually carry along information, right?

Attribute: That's right, Nick. You can declare me with constructor parameters and I'll gladly carry that information right along. Of course, you can only pass constant values to me, but hey, it's information that will ride right along with me and let the developer know what it is with a bit of simple code.

Nick: That's cool. You must be really complicated.

Attribute: No, actually, I'm not. I merely descend from `TCustomAtttribute`, and that is it. The compiler does all the real work of binding me to the RTTI for the given entity I'm attached to.

Nick: Interesting. Well, hey, thanks for your time.

Attribute: No problem – like I said, I'm always happy to come alongside and help out.

10 Using TVirtualInterface

By now you should realize that you need to be programming against interfaces and not implementations. (Didn't I promise you in the first chapter that I'd keep harping on this point?) Interfaces let you write loosely coupled code. And if you don't believe by now that decoupling your code is terribly important, I'd like you to stop reading right now, get a small ball-peen hammer, and keep hitting yourself in the forehead until you change your mind.

So if you have made it this far, you will know that interfaces must be implemented before they can be used. You have to put some code behind an interface to make it do anything. Normally, this is done with an implementing class:

```
type
  ISprocketProcessor = interface
    procedure ProcessSprockets;
  end;


  TSprocketProcessor = class(TInterfacedObject, ISprocketProcessor)
    procedure ProcessSprockets;
  end;
```

But what if you could implement an interface without having a specific class? What if there were a way to implement any interface with a single module of code? What if you could decide at runtime how to implement an interface? Would I even be asking these questions and writing this if those things weren't possible?

So, yes, obviously there is a way. Delphi XE2 introduced a very cool new class called TVirtualInterface. Its purpose is to allow you to descend from it and respond to any interface dynamically. If you think about that for a second, you'll realize that this is pretty powerful. For instance, it's the thing that lets the awesome Delphi Mocks Framework (which we'll talk about in a later chapter) provide a mock implementation of any interface that you pass to it.

As we saw in Chapter 2, normally when you implement an interface, you provide a class that implements it in a specific way – i.e. that implementation becomes static at runtime. There are ways – typically via Dependency Injection – that allow you to choose an implementation, but even then you are limited to a specific set of implementations.

TVirtualInterface allows you to dynamically – i.e. at runtime – determine how an interface will be implemented. I'll start out with some simple examples, and then we'll move to a useful use of TVirtualInterface.

Here's the public interface for TVirtualInterface:

```
  { TVirtualInterface: Creates an implementation of an interface at runtime.
    All methods in the Interface are marshaled through a generic stub function
    that raises the OnInvoke event.}
  TVirtualInterface = class(TInterfacedObject, IInterface)
...
  public
    function QueryInterface(const IID: TGUID; out Obj): HResult; virtual; stdcall;
    { Create an instance of TVirtualInterface that implements the methods of
      an interface.  PIID is the PTypeInfo for the Interface that is to be
      implemented. The Interface must have TypeInfo ($M+). Either inherit from
      IInvokable, or enable TypeInfo for the interface. Because this is an
      TInterfacedObject, it is reference counted and it should not be Freed direc\
tly.
    }
    constructor Create(PIID: PTypeInfo); overload;
    constructor Create(PIID: PTypeInfo; InvokeEvent: TVirtualInterfaceInvokeEvent\
); overload;
    destructor Destroy; override;
    { OnInvoke: Event raised when a method of the implemented interface is called.
      Assign a OnInvoke handler to perform some action on invoked methods.}
    property OnInvoke: TVirtualInterfaceInvokeEvent read FOnInvoke write FOnInvok\
e;
  end;
```

Here are some things to note about the declaration:

- First, you should notice that `TVirtualInterface` descends from `TInterfacedObject` and implements `IInterface`. The three methods of `IInterface` are implemented to allow the class to be properly reference counted like any other interface-implementing class.
- Second, the interface that you want to implement with it needs to have TypeInfo enabled for it. The easiest way to make that happen is to descend your interface from `IInvokable`. Otherwise, you'll need to use the {$M+} switch for your interface. Notice, too, that the comment above the class declaration says what I said earlier – using `TVirtualInterface` will let you, well, do anything you want with an interface at runtime. Cool.
- Finally, note that the class re-declares `QueryInterface` and makes it virtual.

In order to actually make `TVirtualInterface` do something, you need to create a descendant class and provide two things: a constructor and an implementation of the `DoEvent` method.

Here's a `TVirtualInterface` descendant that is as simple an example as I could think of:

```
type
  TSimplestVirtualInterface = class(TVirtualInterface)
    constructor Create(PIID: PTypeInfo);
    procedure DoInvoke(Method: TRttiMethod;  const Args: TArray<TValue>; out Resu\
lt: TValue);
  end;

constructor TSimplestVirtualInterface.Create(PIID: PTypeInfo);
begin
  inherited Create(PIID, DoInvoke);
end;

procedure TSimplestVirtualInterface.DoInvoke(Method: TRttiMethod;
  const Args: TArray<TValue>; out Result: TValue);
begin
  WriteLn('You called a method on an interface');
end;
```

The only thing this will do is to write out to the console – no matter what method you call. You can pretend it implements any interface, and no matter what you call on that interface, it will merely write to the console.

The constructor takes a single parameter, PIID, which is the TypeInfo for the interface you want to implement (That's why the interface in question must have the {M+} switch – again, usually and most easily via IInvokable.). Inside the constructor, a call to a different constructor is made. The PIID parameter is passed in, as is a reference to DoInvoke, which is a method that matches the type TVirtualInterfaceInvokeEvent. Thus, the constructor is basically saying *"Here is the type of information for the interface I'm implementing, and the method you should run whenever a method is called on that interface."*

In our case, the DoInvoke method only does one thing no matter what – writes to the console.

So, for instance, say you declare an interface:

```
type
  IGoStop = interface(IInvokable)
  ['{3B2171B0-D1C3-4A8C-B09E-ACAC4D625E57}']
    procedure Go;
    procedure Stop(aInteger: integer);
  end;
```

And then you run the following code in a console application:

```
GoStop := TSimplestVirtualInterface.Create(TypeInfo(IGoStop)) as IGoStop;
GoStop.Go;
GoStop.Stop(42);
```

the console output will look like this:

```
You called a method on an interface
You called a method on an interface
```

You see the output twice because the code called two methods. It doesn't matter what you call – that output will happen no matter what. It doesn't matter what interface you pass in or what method you call, the result will be the same.

But of course that isn't useful – to be of any use, you need to be able to know what is getting called, what is getting passed in, and respond accordingly.

Well, you can do that, because if you look at the signature of the DoInvoke method, you'll note that when it gets called by the TVirtualInterface.OnInvoke event, it gets passed the RTTI for the method that was called, an array of TValue that contain the interface itself and all the arguments that the method was passed, as well as an out parameter of type TValue that allows you to return a value if the method being called is a function.

So how about we simply use the DoInvoke event to report out what all that information that it receives.

```
procedure TReportingVirtualInterface.DoInvoke(Method: TRttiMethod;
  const Args: TArray<TValue>; out Result: TValue);
var
  Arg: TValue;
  ArgType, ArgName: string;
  TempKind: TTypeKind;
begin
  Write('You called the ', Method.Name, ' method ');
  if Length(Args) > 1 then
  begin
    Writeln('and it has ', Length(Args) - 1,' parameters:');
    for Arg in Args do
    begin
      TempKind := Arg.Kind;
      if TempKind <> tkInterface then
      begin
        ArgName := Arg.ToString;
        ArgType := Arg.TypeInfo.Name;
```

```
      Writeln(ArgName, ' which is of the type ', ArgType);
    end;
  end;
end else
begin
  Writeln(' and it has no parameters.');
end;
end;
```

This code simply looks over and reports out about the Method and Args parameters that get passed in when the interface is invoked. The very first item in the array is always type information about the interface itself, and the rest are the parameters, in order, as they were passed in. Here, the code simply reports out their values and types, but of course, you can process them as you please.

Again, that is interesting information, but it's just a step towards understanding how TVirtualInferface works. Let's create something that actually does what we want it to.

Here's a basic interface:

```
type
  IActuallyUseful = interface
  ['{16F01BF0-961F-4461-AEBE-B1ACB8D3F0F4}']
    procedure SayHello;
    function ReverseString(aString: string): string;
    function Multiply(x, y: integer): integer;
  end;
```

Then, below is the DoInvoke method for a TActuallyUseful class that will actually do what the interface purports to do:

```
procedure TActuallyUseful.DoInvoke(Method: TRttiMethod;
  const Args: TArray<TValue>; out Result: TValue);
begin
  if UpperCase(Method.Name) = 'SAYHELLO' then
  begin
    WriteLn('Hello World!');
  end else
  begin
    if UpperCase(Method.Name) = 'REVERSESTRING' then
    begin
      Result := ReverseString(Args[1].AsString)
    end else
    begin
```

```
    if UpperCase(Method.Name) = 'MULTIPLY' then
    begin
        Result := Args[1].AsInteger * Args[2].AsInteger;
    end else
    begin
      raise Exception.Create('Bad Parameter name was passed in to the DoInvoke \
method');
    end;
  end;
 end;
end;
```

This code should be fairly self-explanatory. It simply checks for the name of the method that was called and then executes code using the parameter information passed in the Args parameter. If the call is a function, the Result parameter is used to return a value.

You should remember that the initial item in the Args array (that is, the one at the "zero-eth" position) is the interface type itself. The code above also makes assumptions about the number and types of the parameters. Since the code can only be invoked by the methods declared on IActuallyUseful interface, the code can make safe assumptions about the types and order of the parameters.

Now all of this code above is fairly straight-forward – we are basically simulating an implementing class in our examples. Nothing is truly dynamic. The code so far merely shows simple examples of how TVirtualInterface works in a fairly static way. You should now be able to see how you could dynamically implement an interface using a TVirtualInterface descendant.

10.1 A Slightly Better TVirtualInterface

So far, all we've looked at is demo code. I can't think of any reason why you'd actually, in the real world, implement an interface that way. But it serves to show you how TVirtualInterface works and how you can get it to do what you want.

Now TVirtualInterface is a cool class, but as is, it's a little clumsy to use. How about we write a descendant class that does most of the "under the hood" work for you and makes it really easy to dynamically create a virtual interface?

Back in the chapter on Generics, I tried to get you to "think generically" and how generics (or as I prefer to think of them, parameterized types) are useful in more ways than just collections and lists. Well, I got to looking at TVirtualInterface and I thought, "*You know, here's a class that actually requires type information about a given type, and in order for it to do anything useful, you have to give it a type in the constructor, so hmmm.*" And perhaps you can guess where I went from there.

So, consider the following class declaration:

```
type

TVirtualInterfaceEx<T: IInvokable> = class(TVirtualInterface)
protected
  procedure DoInvoke(Method: TRttiMethod;  const Args: TArray<TValue>; out Result\
: TValue);
  procedure DoInvokeImpl(Method: TRttiMethod;  const Args: TArray<TValue>; out Re\
sult: TValue); virtual; abstract;
public
  constructor Create;
end;
```

This is a pretty simple descendant for TVirtualInterface. The most obvious thing is that it takes a parameterized type T that is constrained to be an interface descending from IInvokable. That enables you to explicitly declare what interface TVirtualInterfaceEx is going to implement. You should notice, too, that TVirtualInterfaceEx is an abstract class, as the DoInvokeImpl method is abstract.

So once you have the parameterized type, you know everything you need to implement the interface. As you know from the previous section, the thing you need to do is to provide an implementation of DoInvoke. TVirtualInterfaceEx employs the technique whereby you implement the interface in the base class and provide a "real" implementation in a separate method invoked by the base class. So the implementation looks like this:

```
constructor TVirtualInterfaceEx<T>.Create;
begin
  inherited Create(TypeInfo(T), DoInvoke);
end;

procedure TVirtualInterfaceEx<T>.DoInvoke(Method: TRttiMethod;  const Args: TArra\
y<TValue>; out Result: TValue);
begin
  DoInvokeImpl(Method, Args, Result);
end;
```

The constructor is pretty simple – it is parameter-less and calls a sibling constructor, passing in the TypeInfo for your interface and the DoInvoke method which is of type TVirtualInterfaceInvokeEvent. The code for the DoInvoke method simply calls the DoInvokeImpl method, which, because it is abstract, descendant classes must override.

Thus, to use this class, all you need to do is to descend from it and provide an interface as a parameterized type and an implementation for DoInvokeImpl. So if we wanted to implement the IActuallyUseful interface from the previous example, all we need to do is:

```
TActuallyUsefulEx = class(TVirtualInterfaceEx<IActuallyUseful>)
protected
  procedure DoInvokeImpl(Method: TRttiMethod;  const Args: TArray<TValue>; out Re\
sult: TValue); override;
end;
```

implementing DoInvokeImpl with the same code that was in the DoInvoke event of the TActuallyUseful class.

This isn't anything really fancy, but I liked it because it simplified the process of creating virtual interface implementations and provided another example of a good use for parameterized types. I also like what I mentioned previously – that it clearly declares what interface it is implementing.

10.2 An Actually Useful Example

Okay, enough with the not-all-that-useful examples. I mean, the previous examples were illustrative, but not really "real-world useful."

The true usefulness of TVirtualInterface occurs when you use it to create code where you have no idea what interface the user of your code is going to try to implement. All the examples so far have shown only implementing classes where you do know which interface is being used. The exception so far is the TReportingVirtualInterface example which reports information on any interface you pass to it. Since we have proven that you can use TVirtualInterface to do something useful, let's take it a step further.

A practical use of TVirtualInterface is to create a mocking library for unit testing. I've mentioned previously the Delphi Mocks Framework by Vince Parrett of FinalBuilder fame (We'll be covering that framework extensively in a later chapter.). Another excellent implementation of a mocking framework (as well as a bunch of other very innovative and interesting stuff) is by Stefan Glienke as part of his DSharp framework. Both of these use TVirtualInterface to provide a mock implementation for any interface (though the DSharp code implements its own version of TVirtualInterface that works with Delphi XE – very cool). Both, of course, allow you to pass them any interface, and they'll happily mock your interface for unit testing purposes. So why not do an example here of a very simple mocking object that you can actually use if you want?

10.3 ISimpleStub

In the Unit Testing chapter, I will discuss "The Vocabulary of Unit Testing." In it I'll describe fully the distinction between a stub and a mock. There, you'll see that a "stub" is "a fake that has no effect on the passing or failing of the test, and that exists purely to allow the test to run." So how about we build a universal stub – a class that can pretend to be any interface you want, and not do anything at all. That can't be that tough, can it?

Well, we already have a class that can implement an interface, but we need to find a way for that class to actually *be* the interface. If you want a stub, the stub has to actually be the interface type you are trying to stub out, right?

First, since we always code against abstractions, let's declare an interface:

```
ISimpleStub<T> = interface
['{6AA7C2F0-E62F-497B-9A77-04D6F369A288}']
  function InterfaceToCall: T;
end;
```

And then let's implement it with a descendant of TVirtualInterfaceEx<T>:

```
TSimpleStub<T: IInvokable> = class(TVirtualInterfaceEx<T>, ISimpleStub<T>)
protected
  procedure DoInvokeImpl(Method: TRttiMethod;  const Args: TArray<TValue>; out Re\
sult: TValue); override;
public
  function InterfaceToCall: T;
end;
```

Because TSimpleStub<T> descends from TVirtualInterfaceEx<T>, it can implement any interface you pass to it. It thus overrides DoInvokeImpl from TVirtualInterfaceEx<T> as well as implementing InterfaceToCall from ISimpleStub<T>.

First, let's look at DoInvokeImpl:

```
procedure TSimpleStub<T>.DoInvokeImpl(Method: TRttiMethod; const Args: TArray<TVa\
lue>; out Result: TValue);
begin
  // Since this is a pure stub, don't do anything!
end;
```

Not much to see here – it doesn't do anything. And for a stub, that is fine. That's exactly what stubs are supposed to do – nothing. We don't care what happens when the methods get called; you just need to actually be able to call them in your testing code.

That's where the InterfaceToCall function comes in. The class knows about the type of interface being stubbed because we are passing that type in as a parameterized type. The class itself knows how to implement that interface. There has to be a way to get an actual reference to that implemented interface, right?

```
function TSimpleStub<T>.InterfaceToCall: T;
var
  pInfo : PTypeInfo;
begin
  pInfo := TypeInfo(T);
  if QueryInterface(GetTypeData(pInfo).Guid, Result) <> 0 then
  begin
    raise Exception.CreateFmt('Sorry, TSimpleStub<T> is unable to cast %s to its \
interface ', [string(pInfo.Name)]);
  end;
end;
```

Since TSimpleStub<T> knows the type that T is, you can call QueryInterface on the type information about T itself to get a reference to the interface in question. And of course, once you have that, you can pass that reference anywhere you need to stub out the interface – normally as part of unit testing.

So now you can safely call methods on the stubbed interface. For instance, given this interface:

```
IActuallyUseful = interface(IInvokable)
  ['{16F01BF0-961F-4461-AEBE-B1ACB8D3F0F4}']
  procedure SayHello;
  function ReverseString(aString: string): string;
  function Multiply(x, y: integer): integer;
end;

Writeln('Implementing a TSimpleStub');
SimpleStub := TSimpleStub<IActuallyUseful>.Create;
WriteLn('Nothing should appear between this and the next statement');
SimpleStub.InterfaceToCall.SayHello;
SimpleStub.InterfaceToCall.Multiply(4, 4);
SimpleStub.InterfaceToCall.ReverseString('blah');
WriteLn('Nothing should appear between this and the above statement');
WriteLn;
```

Nothing happens when you call the interface methods, but that's by design: stubs should do nothing. What you can do is call them as part of your unit testing:

```
begin
...
MyClassUnderTest := TSprocketThatTakesAnIWhatever.Create(SimpleStub.InterfaceToCa\
ll)
...
end;
```

10.4 TSimpleMock

Okay, so there's a useful, dynamic way to use `TVirtualInterface`. `TSimpleStub<T>` will work great for a stub that you expect absolutely nothing from. But sometimes you need a fake interface that does something more than just exist, and when that is the case, you are creating a mock. In the unit testing chapter, I'll define a mock as *a fake that keeps track of the behavior of the Class Under Test and passes or fails the test based on that behavior.* Thus, a mock needs to do more than exist like a stub – it needs to behave in a way that you can define. So how about we take 'TSimpleMock

One of the most common things that a mock interface does is to respond with "this" when passed "that". How about we create a simple mock class that lets you define a specific response to a method call?

First, of course, is an interface to code against:

```
ISimpleMock<T> = interface(ISimpleStub<T>)
['{9619542B-A53B-4C0C-B915-45ED140E6479}']
  procedure AddExpectation(aCallName: string; aReturnValue: TValue);
end;
```

The interface augments (remember, "inherits from" is not quite right with interfaces) `ISimpleStub<T>` and adds the `AddExpectation` method. This is the method that we'll use to tell the mock how to respond when an interface method gets called.

Here's the implementing class:

```
TSimpleMock<T: IInvokable> = class(TSimpleStub<T>, ISimpleMock<T>)
private
  FActions: TDictionary<string, TValue>;
protected
  procedure DoInvokeImpl(Method: TRttiMethod;  const Args: TArray<TValue>; out Re\
sult: TValue); override;
public
  constructor Create;
  destructor Destroy; override;
  procedure AddExpectation(aCallName: string; aReturnValue: TValue);
end;
```

The first thing to notice is that TSimpleMock<T> inherits from TSimpleStub<T>, thus enabling it to be any interface it wants to be. And of course it also implements the AddExpectation method. It takes as parameters the name of the method on the interface that you can call, as well as a return value for when that method gets called. In this way you can define the behavior of the mock class however you want.

This very simple mocking example assumes that you are going to be mocking only function calls as methods on an interface. Within the confines of our simple example, it doesn't make sense to mock procedures – they basically don't do anything as far as the simple example is concerned. As we'll see, a full-featured mock framework is able to keep track of whether a procedure is called, how many times it does get called, and other things associated with procedures. This simple example also doesn't care what parameters you pass in, it will merely return a value whenever the named method is called. Remember, this is a simple – but useful in specific situations – example.

The implementation of TSimpleMock<T> is pretty, well, simple. Internally, it uses a TDictionary<TKey, TValue> to keep track of the method calls and the resulting responses that are added via the AddExpectation call. Here is the implementation of AddExpectation :

```
procedure TSimpleMock<T>.AddExpectation(const aCallName: string; aReturnValue: TV\
alue);
begin
  FActions.Add(aCallName, aReturnValue);
end;
```

When you add an expectation, the class keeps track of it. When you then call that method on the interface, it is able to retrieve the expected return value from the dictionary and return it:

```
procedure TSimpleMock<T>.DoInvokeImpl(Method: TRttiMethod; const Args: TArray<TVa\
lue>; out Result: TValue);
begin
  Result := FActions[Method.Name];
end;
```

The obvious shortcoming here is no error handling – you'll get an exception if you try to call a method on the interface that doesn't have an expectation entry. Another shortcoming is that the parameters passed mean nothing – a real mocking framework would be able to provide specific responses for specific parameter inputs. I'll leave correcting this problem as an exercise for the reader.

So now, when we exercise this class, it will actually return stuff that you tell it to:

This code:

```
WriteLn('IActuallyUseful with ISimpleMock');
SimpleMock := TSimpleMock<IActuallyUseful>.Create;
SimpleMock.AddExpectation('Multiply', 99);
SimpleMock.AddExpectation('ReverseString', 'This is actually working');
WriteLn(SimpleMock.InterfaceToCall.Multiply(6, 7));
WriteLn(SimpleMock.InterfaceToCall.ReverseString('This does not matter'));
WriteLn;
```

has the following output:

Note that the responses are not what you think they would be based on the parameters (you think that 6 times 7 would return 42), but what you told them to be in the AddExpectation call.

Now, you can use ISimpleMock<T> to provide specific feedback for a given method call. Maybe you have an interface method that returns a Boolean value that you want to test. You can use ISimpleMock<IInterfaceWithBooleanMethod> to test what happens when the method returns True as well as when that method returns False.

10.5 Conclusion

Okay, so there you have it: A useful implementation of TVirtualInterface. Though the above examples are really simple, they can actually be used in real world testing – particularly the ISimpleStub<T> implementation. Stubbing is common in unit testing, and even though it is a very basic implementation, it can be used to stub out any interface.

None of this is useful if you know what interface you need and how you are going to implement it. But there are cases when you don't know what interface you will need for a particular problem, and you need to be able to flex to whatever interface the situation calls for. Mocking and stubbing are perfect examples. That's a powerful and useful thing to be able to do. Hopefully this chapter has helped you see that.

11 Introduction to Dependency Injection

11.1 Introduction

Dependency Injection is a very powerful and important coding technique. The idea became popular as the notion of "Inversion of Control" after Martin Fowler wrote an article entitled "Inversion of Control Containers and the Dependency Injection Pattern"[1], and since then the notion has advanced rapidly, spawning numerous frameworks, books, and articles describing how to use the powerful and essential technique.

Inversion of Control is the notion that rather than a class creating the things that it needs, it should instead "ask" for those things, receiving them either via a constructor, a property, or a field. Dependency Injection is just a coding technique driven by inversion of control, though there are frameworks that help to support its use. To truly get the concept of Dependency Injection, though, we should talk about some general topics. There are a few things that need to be accepted and understood before Dependency Injection can become infused into your development process.

11.2 What is a Dependency?

A dependency is something that you depend on. That's a bit of a snarky answer to the question posed by the section header, but it does get to the point: It's quite common for one class to depend on another. And if one class depends on another, then those classes are coupled together. Class A depends on Class B when you can't compile Class A without Class B. That's really what coupling amounts to – and coupled code is bad, as we know.

How does a dependency get created? Most commonly, they get created any time you create one class inside of another. For example:

---

[1] http://martinfowler.com/articles/injection.html

```
procedure TWidget.SendWidget;
var
  WidgetSender: TWidgetSender;
begin
  WidgetSender := TWidgetSender.Create;
  try
    WidgetSender.SendWidget(Self);
  finally
    WidgetSender.Free;
  end;
end;
```

Given the above code, the TWidget class has a strict, tightly-coupled dependency on TWidgetSender. You can't create and use a TWidget without also pulling in and using TWidgetSender (and only TWidgetSender). TWidget is irrevocably dependent on TWidgetSender. The unit that TWidget is declared in has to use the unit that TWidgetSender is in. They are hopelessly intertwined and connected to each other. You have no flexibility in the way widgets are sent – they are sent the way that TWidgetSender sends them, and that's it.

The point here is: Don't do that. Don't create dependencies. And of course, at this point you might ask – how do I not create a dependency?

We'll get to that, but first, let's discuss an important thing that pertains to this whole notion of dependencies and not creating them – the Law of Demeter.

11.3 The Law of Demeter (LoD)

What exactly is the Law of Demeter, you ask? The strict definition goes like this:

A method of an object may only call methods of:

- The object itself.
- An argument of the method.
- Any object created within the method.
- Any direct properties/fields of the object.

That's a bit formal, so here's an example:

Let's say you go into a store. You buy a bunch of stuff, and the total is $25. When you go to pay, what do you do? If you are believer in the Law of Demeter, you pull out your wallet and give the $25 to the clerk – just the money, nothing more.

But no, you are a scofflaw and fear not the deep coupling of your wallet to other people and thus you think the Law of Demeter is for weaker people, so you pull out your wallet and hand the whole thing over to the clerk and let him decide what to do for the payment.

Sure, you intended to pay with cash, but instead the clerk takes your wallet, uses a credit card to pay for the stuff, drops your library card on the floor, runs your BuyMore loyalty card through a degaussing machine, and draws a mustache on the picture of your wife. You paid for the stuff, but wow, what a mess!

That is why you should follow the Law of Demeter. Its basic premise is that you should only hand over (and on the other side, only ask for) exactly what you need to hand over (or ask for). Things should be linked together with as thin a string as possible. The Venn diagram illustrating the connections between your classes should have as small an overlap as can be managed. In this example, you might not even want the clerk to know you have a wallet.

Or in another example, you wouldn't let the paperboy search around your house for spare change, right? Same principle – keep the interfaces (ha!) between two things as thin and lean as possible.

11.4 A Design Example

For instance, in code, you may have a `Transaction` class that needs a form of payment to be completed. And hey, look! The `Customer` class has different Forms of Payment, so you pass a `Customer` to the `Transaction`. At first all is well, because you are very careful and all you do is grab the Form of Payment from the customer and use it. What could possibly go wrong?

But a few months pass, and that (cough, cough) "less experienced" developer comes along and is doing some maintenance work on the `Transaction class`. He says, "Hey look! Here's a `Customer` object! I think I'll change his address here instead of over there!" and suddenly all heck breaks loose. Pretty soon, you are fixing a bug in the `Transaction` class and `Customer` data changes. You fix a `Customer` bug and access violations start flying when you try to commit transactions to the database. The next thing you know, changing a `Customer` address is sending major cash bonuses to your office cleaning service, and before you know it, there is no end to the havoc wreaked by that little `Customer` object innocently sitting in the `Transaction` class.

The right thing to do, of course, is to simply pass the Form of Payment itself, or better yet, forget the Form of Payment and pass in just the money itself in some form. The idea is that your classes should ask for a little as possible, and refuse to accept more than they need. If you have code like this –

```
Transaction.Customer.FormOfPayment.CreditCardNumber.ProcessCreditCard;
```

– that is, code that seems to drill down deep into a class hierarchy – then you probably deserve a ticket from the cops for breaking the Law of Demeter. You've gone searching down a rabbit hole for something that you should have just asked for to start with.

The classic quote in computer science is "Only talk to your friends, and never talk to strangers." "Mind your own business" comes to mind as well.

Or let's put it in even starker terms: Pretend that every class you write is a pristine clean room with no germs, dirt, or any other yucky stuff in it – and that you plan on keeping it that way. Are you going to let some delivery guy who just tramped through a horse barn while sneezing because of the ebola virus just walk into your room and hand you a package? Heck no! You are going to make him shower, scrub, de-sanitize, purify, and otherwise delouse himself before entering. Sheesh, you should probably make this guy put on some sort of bio-hazard suit before you let him in. Or even better still, don't let him in at all, and only let him pass in whatever he's trying to give you via some secure slot in the door.

Here's another way to think about it. Imagine you have a six year-old, and her seventh birthday is coming up. You need a cake. So you decide to bake one with her! Well, that's sweet and everything, but you can figure out what your kitchen will look like afterwards – flour everywhere, icing all over you and the counters, a general big mess.

You can, of course, avoid that by going to the bakery and buying a cake. Or better yet, have the cake delivered right to your house.

It's like that with code: If you create things yourself, you can end up with a big mess. But if, instead, your classes have what they need delivered to them ready-made and ready to go, then things are a lot cleaner.

And that is precisely where the basic notion of Dependency Injection lies.

11.5 Law of Demeter in Delphi

Delphi and the Law of Demeter can be good friends. Here are some pointers to help out in your Delphi code:

- Limit the scope of your uses clauses. If you can put an item in the uses clause of the implementation, do so.
- Use strict private and strict protected. This will limit you from the temptation to make classes "friends" of each other in the same unit.
- As noted above, any time you have a chain of "dotted" properties in a single line, you should examine this for violations of the Law of Demeter.
- Any time you are creating a lot of temporary objects, this might indicate unnecessary dependencies.
- Check your constructors – if they are creating anything or taking a lot of other classes as parameters, then the same thing applies: the possibility of too much coupling.
- Note that these aren't iron-clad rules but rather suggestions of examination and consideration. It need not become a "dot counting exercise." The idea is to reduce coupling and thus limit the effect any one modification can have on the system as a whole.

One of the main reasons to follow the Law of Demeter is to write code and code modules that are loosely coupled. Loosely coupled modules have minimal interactions with other modules and thus have minimal effect on those other modules. Change something in a loosely coupled module and the chances of breaking something in another module are slim. If you have a minimal connection to another module, then you can only cause minimal bugs in that module.

And "minimal bugs" is a phrase to warm the heart of us all, no?

11.6 A Step-by-Step Code Example

Okay, so what does this all mean for the way you should code? Let's go through a simple example that starts the "old-fashioned way" of doing things and moves step-by-step toward a loosely coupled solution that illustrates the basics of Dependency Injection.

Consider the following code:

```
unit Step1;

interface

type
  TOrder = class
    function Amount: integer;
  end;

  TOrderValidator = class
    procedure ValidateOrder(aOrder: TOrder);
  end;

  TOrderProcessor = class
  private
    FOrderValidator: TOrderValidator;
  public
    constructor Create;
    destructor Destroy; override;
    procedure ProcessOrder(aOrder: TOrder);
  end;

procedure ProcessOrders;

implementation

uses
```

```
    System.SysUtils
  ;

procedure ProcessOrders;
var
  OrderProcessor: TOrderProcessor;
begin
  OrderProcessor := TOrderProcessor.Create;
  try
    OrderProcessor.ProcessOrder(TOrder.Create);
  finally
    OrderProcessor.Free;
  end;
end;

function TOrder.Amount: integer;
begin
  Result := Random(1000) + 1
end;

constructor TOrderProcessor.Create;
begin
  FOrderValidator := TOrderValidator.Create;
end;

destructor TOrderProcessor.Destroy;
begin
  FOrderValidator.Free;
  inherited;
end;

procedure TOrderProcessor.ProcessOrder(aOrder: TOrder);
begin
  FOrderValidator.ValidateOrder(aOrder);
end;

procedure TOrderValidator.ValidateOrder(aOrder: TOrder);
begin
  WriteLn('Order is valid for $' + IntToStr(aOrder.Amount));
end;

end.
```

This code represents the way that things have commonly been done in the past before people became more aware of Dependency Injection. There are three classes: TOrder, TOrderProcessor, and TOrderValidator. None of them does anything particularly interesting – they are designed merely for illustrative purposes. TOrderProcessor processes orders and validates them with TOrderValidator. We won't look too closely at the TOrder class – it is there to give TOrderProcessor something to do. What we will do, however, is look at the relationship between TOrderValidator and TOrderProcessor.

Take a look at the constructor for TOrderProcessor. In it, we create an instance of TOrderValidator. We can't compile TOrderProcessor without compiling TOrderValidator. We are, therefore, tightly coupled to TOrderValidator. We must use that instance of TOrderProcessor and no other. If we want to change the way orders are validated, then we'll have a heck of a time replacing TOrderValidator. Any bugs in TOrderValidator can directly affect TOrderProcessor. In our simple example, it only has one method, but imagine a more complex situation where the interface of TOrderValidator was tied to a specific implementation and had many method calls that ranged about the application. Replacing it could be very difficult.

In addition, testing TOrderValidator will be difficult. Imagine if TOrderValidator created a large set of its own dependencies or connected to external resources or otherwise complicated the processing of orders. In order to test TOrderValidator, you'd have to take on those additional dependencies just to run tests.

So, let's take a simple step. Instead of hard-coding the creation of TOrderValidator in the constructor of TOrderProcessor, let's defer the construction of TOrderValidator and pass an existing instance of TOrderValidator to the constructor of TOrderProcessor. Here's an updated version of our code that does this:

```
unit Step2;

interface

type
  TOrder = class
    function Amount: integer;
  end;

  TOrderValidator = class
    procedure ValidateOrder(aOrder: TOrder);
  end;

  TOrderProcessor = class
  private
    FOrderValidator: TOrderValidator;
  public
```

```
    constructor Create(aOrderValidator: TOrderValidator);
    destructor Destroy; override;
    procedure ProcessOrder(aOrder: TOrder);
  end;

procedure ProcessOrders2;

implementation

uses
    System.SysUtils
    ;

procedure ProcessOrders2;
var
  Order: TOrder;
  OrderProcessor: TOrderProcessor;
begin
  OrderProcessor := TOrderProcessor.Create(TOrderValidator.Create);
  try
    Order := TOrder.Create;
    try
      OrderProcessor.ProcessOrder(Order);
    finally
      Order.Free;
    end;
  finally
    OrderProcessor.Free;
  end;
end;

function TOrder.Amount: integer;
begin
  Result := Random(1000) + 1
end;

{ TOrderProcessor }

constructor TOrderProcessor.Create(aOrderValidator: TOrderValidator);
begin
  inherited Create;
  FOrderValidator := aOrderValidator;
```

```
end;

destructor TOrderProcessor.Destroy;
begin
  FOrderValidator.Free;
  inherited Destroy;
end;

procedure TOrderProcessor.ProcessOrder(aOrder: TOrder);
begin
  FOrderValidator.ValidateOrder(aOrder);
end;

procedure TOrderValidator.ValidateOrder(aOrder: TOrder);
begin
  WriteLn('Order is valid for $' + IntToStr(aOrder.Amount));
end;

end.
```

Now, the TOrderProcessor class takes a TOrderValidator as a constructor parameter. Note, too, that it takes ownership of that class and destroys it in its destructor. In doing this, we get only a small improvement. We are not strictly tied to TOrderValidator, as we could pass in a descendant class. That gives us more flexibility and slightly less coupling. It's not much, but it is something.

The other thing to note, as well, is that we have "pushed back" the creation of TOrderValidator closer to the main root of the application. Keep an eye on that as we go forward – the notion of pushing back creation of objects is a key factor in Dependency Injection.

Let's decouple things even further. Consider the following:

```
unit Step3;

interface

type
  TOrder = class
    function Amount: integer;
  end;

  IOrderValidator = interface
  ['{4CCA1F87-21C2-4755-9E6F-8573B909CE11}']
  procedure ValidateOrder(aOrder: TOrder);
```

```
  end;

  TOrderValidator = class(TInterfacedObject, IOrderValidator)
    procedure ValidateOrder(aOrder: TOrder);
  end;

  TOrderProcessor = class
  private
    FOrderValidator: IOrderValidator;
  public
    constructor Create(aOrderValidator: IOrderValidator);
    procedure ProcessOrder(aOrder: TOrder);
  end;

procedure ProcessOrders3;

implementation

uses
      System.SysUtils
    ;

procedure ProcessOrders3;
var
  Order: TOrder;
  OrderProcessor: TOrderProcessor;
begin
  OrderProcessor := TOrderProcessor.Create(TOrderValidator.Create);
  try
    Order := TOrder.Create;
    try
      OrderProcessor.ProcessOrder(Order);
    finally
      Order.Free;
    end;
  finally
    OrderProcessor.Free;
  end;
end;

function TOrder.Amount: integer;
begin
```

```
  Result := Random(1000) + 1
end;

constructor TOrderProcessor.Create(aOrderValidator: IOrderValidator);
begin
  inherited Create;
  FOrderValidator := aOrderValidator;
end;


procedure TOrderProcessor.ProcessOrder(aOrder: TOrder);
begin
  FOrderValidator.ValidateOrder(aOrder);
end;

{ TOrderValidator }

procedure TOrderValidator.ValidateOrder(aOrder: TOrder);
begin
  WriteLn('Order is valid for $' + IntToStr(aOrder.Amount));
end;

end.
```

Here's a bullet list of the things that have happened:

- We've declared an interface called IOrderValidator that has all the methods needed to do the work of validating an order. Now, we don't care what class implements IOrderValidator, we just know that we can call ValidateOrder on an order and it will get validated.
- TOrderProcessor now stores a reference to an interface internally instead of an object reference.
- TOrderValidator now descends from TInterfacedObject, thus providing the reference counting required by interfaces.
- We no longer have to worry about ownership. Because interfaces are reference counted, we don't need the destructor on TOrderProcessor any more to free the instance.

Thus, in Step 3, we have decoupled TOrderProcessor from the class TOrderValidator and are coupled to IOrderValidator instead. As we discussed in the interfaces chapter, you have to couple to something, and an interface is the thinnest, leanest thing you can couple to. So in this step, we've decoupled further, but not completely. We still have to create a class that implements IOrderValidator.

However, we have made a significant step: we have inverted the control of order validation by making the decision about how orders are validated outside of the TOrderProcessor class. The decision about what implementation to use gets made in the call to ProcessOrder3. TOrderProcessor doesn't care anymore about what implementation validates orders. This is a big step.

In addition, we have done the most basic and important kind of Dependency Injection: **Constructor Injection**. We have created an order validator outside the scope of TOrderProcessor and then "injected" that implementation into TOrderProcessor via its constructor. TOrderProcessor has been decoupled from any particular implementation of order validation, giving us the freedom to use any implementation we want. In addition, we've satisfied the Law of Demeter by passing to TOrderValidator the smallest thing we can – an interface.

However, we are still tied closely to a specific implementation – we've just pushed that implementation decision back to the call to ProcessOrders3. There, we are still hard-coding a call to TOrderValidator. It's decoupled from TOrderProcessor, but we've just moved that coupling closer to the program "root" – that is, the very first command executed by our application. In Delphi applications, that is the first line of the DPR file. This is one of the principles of Dependency Injection – to push the creation of objects as far back towards the application root as possible.

So the next step we'll take is to isolate the interface. Currently, in our simple example, we have everything in the same unit. What we'll do next is to separate the interface out from the code that implements that interface. This will ensure that the interface isn't found in the same unit as the implementation, thus further separating and decoupling our code. When we do that, though, we need to declare an interface to an order – IOrder – so that our IOrderValidator interface is no longer coupled to the specific implementation found in TOrder, but rather to an interface. See how this is contagious – in a good way? By isolating things both via code and via putting things in separate units, we can start to clearly see a path towards more decoupled code.

As a result, we get a unit called OrderInterfaces.pas that looks like this:

```
unit OrderInterfaces;

interface

type

  IOrder = interface
  ['{B4680E66-2642-40CC-B4EB-EEE9172F49B1}']
    function Amount: integer;
  end;

  IOrderValidator = interface
  ['{4CCA1F87-21C2-4755-9E6F-8573B909CE11}']
    procedure ValidateOrder(aOrder: IOrder);
  end;
```

```
implementation

end.
```

and an **implementation** that looks like this:

```
unit Step4;

interface

uses
     OrderInterfaces
   ;

type
  TOrder = class(TInterfacedObject, IOrder)
    function Amount: integer;
  end;

  TOrderValidator = class(TInterfacedObject, IOrderValidator)
    procedure ValidateOrder(aOrder: IOrder);
  end;

  TOrderProcessor = class
  private
    FOrderValidator: IOrderValidator;
  public
    constructor Create(aOrderValidator: IOrderValidator);
    procedure ProcessOrder(aOrder: IOrder);
  end;

procedure ProcessOrders4;

implementation

uses
     System.SysUtils
   ;

procedure ProcessOrders4;
var
```

```
  Order: IOrder;
  OrderProcessor: TOrderProcessor;
begin
  OrderProcessor := TOrderProcessor.Create(TOrderValidator.Create);
  try
    Order := TOrder.Create;
    OrderProcessor.ProcessOrder(Order);
  finally
    OrderProcessor.Free;
  end;
end;


function TOrder.Amount: integer;
begin
  Result := Random(1000) + 1
end;


constructor TOrderProcessor.Create(aOrderValidator: IOrderValidator);
begin
  inherited Create;
  FOrderValidator := aOrderValidator;
end;


procedure TOrderProcessor.ProcessOrder(aOrder:IOrder);
begin
  FOrderValidator.ValidateOrder(aOrder);
end;


procedure TOrderValidator.ValidateOrder(aOrder: IOrder);
begin
  WriteLn('Order is valid for $' + IntToStr(aOrder.Amount));
end;


end.
```

Things to note:

- Both TOrder and TOrderValidator implement interfaces.
- TOrderProcessor only takes interfaces and doesn't deal with any concrete classes at all.
- Instantiation of TOrder and TOrderValidator can be done without concern about freeing them because they are handled as interfaces. This makes coding and memory handling simpler and less prone to error.

- Because IOrder and IOrderValidator are interfaces, it is much easier (but not easy enough yet, as we'll see later) to replace the existing implementation with another one. All that is needed is a class that implements IOrderValidator, and IOrderProcessor will be happy. That new class can easily replace the existing class in only one place.

We've done a good job of decoupling the classes from each other. We've moved creation "back" closer to the application root and made it so that we can replace an implementation more easily if desired. Let's turn our attention to the place where all that creation is still taking place – the ProcessOrdersX method.

11.7 The Dependency Injection Container

Remember, every time you call Create, you are not only creating an instance, you are also creating a dependency. As we slowly push the creation of all these classes back as far as we can towards the very root of our application, the more decoupled the downstream things can be. And if you haven't figured it out yet, we're going to try to push the creation of objects so far back into the bowels of your application that you can't even really see it. That way, everything is downstream from the actual creation of objects, letting you easily decouple your code because you'll mainly be coding against interfaces, and leaving the creation of the code to processes at the very root of your application.

So what is this method by which your classes will be created out of sight? The technique is usually called a Dependency Injection Container. The Delphi Spring Framework includes a container that is easy to use and is very powerful. We'll look at the basics of using it in the rest of this chapter and at its advanced use in the next chapter.

A Dependency Injection container is a special class that holds information about the interfaces you use and the classes that implement them. You can register a given class as implementing a given interface. Once registered, you can retrieve an interface with an instantiated implementation. Why is this cool and good? Because when retrieving an instantiated interface, *you only need to know about the interface and not about the class implementing it.*

A Dependency Injection Container takes care of creating the class for you via RTTI; you don't ever have to call Create yourself. Thus, you can deal purely with interfaces without ever having to worry about creating anything. And if you aren't creating anything, you can't cause dependencies, and if you can't cause dependencies, then you can't cause deep coupling.

How does all this work? The first thing you do with a container is register classes and interfaces. The code for registering can be found in the Spring.Container unit. Place that unit in the uses clause of the unit where your classes are declared and you can register them. The Container is registered as a singleton called GlobalContainer, and this is the class that you will use to register your classes. In our simple example, we'll register our TOrderValidator class as implementing the IOrderValidator field in the initialization section of the unit as follows:

```
initialization
    GlobalContainer.RegisterType<TOrderValidator>.Implements<IOrderValidato\
r>;
```

The above code basically reads as follows: "In the GlobalContainer, register the TOrderValidator class as implementing the IOrderValidator interface." This way, the container now knows what class it should create when an IOrderValidator is needed. We do the registration in the initialization section to keep it as close to the root of the application as possible; the registration will take place right as the application starts up.

But of course, that is only half the battle. Instead of creating an instance of TOrderValidator ourselves and thus coupling to it, we use what is called the ServiceLocator to grab an implemented instance for IOrderValidator out of the Container. The ServiceLocator is found in the Spring.Services unit and is used as follows:

```
procedure ProcessOrders5;
var
  Order: IOrder;
  OrderValidator: IOrderValidator;
  OrderProcessor: TOrderProcessor;
begin
  OrderValidator := ServiceLocator.GetService<IOrderValidator>;
  OrderProcessor := TOrderProcessor.Create(OrderValidator);
  try
    Order := TOrder.Create;
    OrderProcessor.ProcessOrder(Order);
  finally
    OrderProcessor.Free;
  end;
end;
```

By using the ServiceLocator, we can separate completely from the creation of the class implementing the desired interface. The call to ProcessOrders5 doesn't have a Create call on TOrderValidator. However, we still have things all coupled together in one unit, but when we split everything apart in the next section, we can limit the exposure of our code to only having the units with concrete implementations in the DPR file and the units with the interface declarations as the only units that you need to get the functionality your code requires.

> For now, we'll use the ServiceLocator to create our classes, but in the next chapter, I'm going to argue that we shouldn't even be doing that.

So let's do that in Step6. In Step6, we'll do the following:

1. Place `TOrderValidator` and `TOrder` in the `implementation` section of their own units and registered them as implementing their interfaces with the `GlobalContainer`. Notice something interesting – this results in a unit with *nothing in its interface section*. Wild, huh? If there is no code in a unit's `interface` section, it cannot couple to anything at all. Yet we can still access the code via the `Container`/`ServiceLocator` combination. I wouldn't necessarily recommend doing this in real code, but it is an indicator of how decoupled your code really can be with proper dependency injection techniques.

2. The main unit – `Unit6` – where `TOrderProcessor` resides now only has the `OrderInterfaces` unit in its uses clause, so it can only couple to interfaces now. It cannot connect any more to any concrete implementation. Keeping your `uses` clause as lean as possible is an important part of loose coupling in Delphi.

3. Since the registration takes place in the `initialization` section of the implementing units, and since those units are included in the project, the management of the creation of instances has been pushed back all the way to the very root of the application itself.

4. In order for the `GlobalContainer` to work, it must be built, and so the very first line in the DPR file is `GlobalContainer.Build`. The creation of objects can't be pushed back any farther than that.

Thus, the `uOrder.pas` unit looks like this:

```
unit uOrder;

interface

implementation

uses
    OrderInterfaces
  , Spring.Container
  ;

type

  TOrder = class(TInterfacedObject, IOrder)
    function Amount: integer;
  end;

function TOrder.Amount: integer;
begin
  Result := Random(1000) + 1
end;
```

```
initialization
  GlobalContainer.RegisterType<TOrder>.Implements<IOrder>;

end.
```

Again, note the empty interface section.

The `ProcessOrder` method now looks a lot simpler, as well:

```
unit Step6;

interface

uses
    OrderInterfaces
  ;

type

  TOrderProcessor = class
  private
    FOrderValidator: IOrderValidator;
  public
    constructor Create(aOrderValidator: IOrderValidator);
    procedure ProcessOrder(aOrder: IOrder);
  end;

procedure ProcessOrders6;

implementation

uses
    System.SysUtils
  , Spring.Container
  , Spring.Services
  ;

procedure ProcessOrders6;
var
  Order: IOrder;
  OrderValidator: IOrderValidator;
  OrderProcessor: TOrderProcessor;
begin
```

```
  OrderValidator := ServiceLocator.GetService<IOrderValidator>;
  OrderProcessor := TOrderProcessor.Create(OrderValidator);
  try
    Order := ServiceLocator.GetService<IOrder>;
    OrderProcessor.ProcessOrder(Order);
  finally
    OrderProcessor.Free;
  end;
end;


constructor TOrderProcessor.Create(aOrderValidator: IOrderValidator);
begin
  inherited Create;
  FOrderValidator := aOrderValidator;
end;


procedure TOrderProcessor.ProcessOrder(aOrder: IOrder);
begin
  FOrderValidator.ValidateOrder(aOrder);
end;


end.
```

Notice that the only unit it requires from our library is OrderInterfaces, which contains nothing but interfaces. Thus, our ordering system is completely decoupled, communicating purely with those interfaces and the ServiceLocator. The creation of classes is pushed all the way back to the DPR file itself. Because you no longer need to worry about creating anything, but instead are merely requesting interfaces with implementations, you will actually have a difficult time coupling code together.

At this point, you might be wondering "What should I put in the Container?" Well, here are some rules of thumb that I'd recommend you follow:

- Always code to interfaces, and always register a class against that interface in the container. If you write a class, expose it as an interface and put it into the Container.
- Do not put Runtime Library or other similar code into the container. There's no need for TStringList or TStream to be included in the container. Again, classes you write should go into the container, but proven, stable library classes can be created locally and used normally.
- Whenever you create something, stop and consider if that creation shouldn't be done by the Container. Eventually, you can reduce your Create calls down to the basics of the RTL and nothing more.
- In general, when in doubt, put it into the container. As we'll see in the next chapter, you can even register multiple implementations against a single interface, so the Container is incredibly useful. Things that are incredibly useful should be used, right?

11.8 Conclusion

In this chapter, we covered the very basics of Dependency Injection, including a discussion about the Law of Demeter and how we should keep our coupling as thin as possible. This led to talking about constructor injection as a basic DI technique. An example of decoupling code caused us to use a DI Container to ensure that the creation of objects is done as far away from your "real" code as possible.

In the next chapter we'll look more closely at the Spring Container and what it can do to improve your ability to inject dependencies rather than create them.

12 A Deeper Look at Dependency Injection

Okay, so by now you should have the general idea about what Dependency Injection is. You should understand that one class should avoid directly creating instances of a second class, but instead, defer creation as far back as possible within the application, even to the point of letting a container create your classes for you.

But there's a bit more structure to the notion of Dependency Injection and a lot more that the Spring Container can do for you, so we'll examine both of those things in this chapter.

Let's start with a simple example. Consider this class:

```
type
  TKnight = class
  private
    FWeapon: IWeapon;
  public
    constructor Create(aWeapon: IWeapon)
  end;
```

This is a pretty obvious example of constructor injection. The constructor takes a parameter, aWeapon, indicating that you can give the knight any weapon that he needs. The presence of the parameter on the constructor also is a message to developers that a Knight *must* have a weapon. You can't create a knight without passing him a weapon (and we presume that the constructor fails if aWeapon is nil). Thus, constructor injection should be used to indicate the *required* dependencies that a class has.

As noted above, it is standard practice not to accept nil parameters when constructing an object. If a constructor has a parameter, then that parameter represents a dependency that can never be nil. Thus, TKnight's constructor might look like this:

```
constructor TKnight.Create(aWeapon: IWeapon);
begin
  inherited Create;
  if aWeapon = nil then
  begin
    raise ENoWeaponException.Create('A knight must have a weapon');
  end;
  FWeapon := aWeapon;
end;
```

By doing this, a class can ensure that it is never in an incorrect state. In the case of our knight, a knight should never be without a weapon, and the user of the TKnight class can code as if a weapon always exists.

12.1 Optional Dependencies

Sometimes, however, dependencies are not required. Thus, consider this class:

```
type
  TBasketballPlayer = class
  private
    FBall: IBasketball;
  public
    constructor Create(aBasketball: IBasketball);
  end;
```

At first glance, this looks right – but then you stop to consider that basketball teams require five players and there is only one ball. Thus, you can't create all five players, each with a ball. The dependency of a ball is *optional* in this case. What to do?

12.2 Setter Injection

This is where "Setter Injection" comes in. Instead of passing the dependency in via the constructor where it is required for creating a player, we can instead set the ball for each player as they pass it around:

```
type
  TBasketballPlayer = class
  private
    FBall: IBasketball
  public
    constructor Create;
    property Ball: IBasketball read FBall write FBall;
  end;
```

Now, instead of requiring that a player have the ball, we can create a player and optionally let them have or give up the ball via the Ball property. The ball is not required, but it can be assigned as needed to a given player. Thus, Setter Injection allows a dependency to be externally assigned as desired. Again, the construction of the dependency is done externally, and the dependency is injected into the class, this time via a property.

Note that Setter Injection can also be used to directly set a field value as opposed to a property. However, Field Injection, as it is called, is not a generally recommended technique for the same reasons that you should prefer properties over public fields. In addition, private fields are, well, private, and just as we shouldn't externally change private field as a general rule, we should avoid using the container to do so.

Now consider this case:

```
type
  TKnight = class
  private
    FWeapon: IWeapon;
  public
    constructor Create(aWeapon: IWeapon)
    property Weapon: IWeapon read FWeapon write FWeapon;
  end;
```

Here, we've combined Constructor Injection and Setter injection to indicate that the Weapon dependency is required – it must be passed in via the constructor, but that it is also available for modification. It might be that once you create a knight with a given weapon, you might want to change what weapon that knight is using.

12.3 Method Injection

A third type of Dependency Injection that you might use is Method Injection. Similar to Setter Injection, you instead use a method to assign the dependency. See the following code:

```
type
  TKnight = class
  private
    FWeapon: IWeapon;
  public
    constructor Create(aWeapon: IWeapon)
    procedure Arm(aWeapon: IWeapon);
    property Weapon: TWeapon read FWeapon;
  end;
```

In this code, we use Construction Injection to require that the knight has a weapon, but we provide a method that allows us to give the knight any weapon that we want.

All of techniques ensure that your dependencies are flexible and not hard-coded. They allow you to determine dependencies outside of the class itself. And if your dependencies are injected, that means that your code isn't coupled.

But the question arises – if a dependency is optional, how do we handle that dependency not being present? Well, a real world example might look something like this:

```
type
    TTextProcessor = class
    private
      FText: string;
      FSpellChecker: ISpellChecker;
    public
      constructor Create(aText: string);
      procedure ProcessText;
      property SpellChecker: ISpellChecker read FSpellChecker write FSpellC\
hecker;
    end;

    constructor TTextProcessor.Create(aText: string);
    begin
      inherited Create;
      FText := aText;
      FSpellChecker := nil;
    end;

    procedure TTextProcessor.ProcessText;
    begin
      if SpellChecker <> nil then
      begin
```

```
      FText := SpellChecker.CheckSpelling(FText);
    end;
    // Do something to text?
  end;
```

In the above code, we use Setter Injection to indicate that we can optionally have a spell checker as part of the text processing done by the class. When the time comes, you can check for the presence of a spell checker, and if there is one, use it to spell check the text. If there isn't one, you can process the text without a spell check. This is a simple but effective way to manage your optional dependencies.

There is another way to use Setter Injection. You can use it to allow for a dependency to be changed, but to have the constructor provide a "reasonable default" for the class. Consider this:

```
type
  TKnight = class
  private
    FWeapon: IWeapon;
  public
    constructor Create;
    property Weapon: TWeapon read FWeapon write FWeapon;
  end;

constructor TKnight.Create;
begin
  inherited Create;
  FWeapon := TSword.Create;
end;
```

Here, we have a parameter-less constructor, but the constructor creates a "default" weapon, a sword, for the knight. However, because of the presence of the Weapon property, the developer can change the weapon that the knight uses. This is a subtle but important difference in the use of Constructor Injection.

Thus, we can state the following general rules:

1. Use Constructor Injection to indicate that a dependency is required. Constructor Injection can enforce the presence of a given dependency by requiring that the class be constructed with valid instances of the dependencies indicated in the parameters.
2. Use Setter Injection to indicate that a dependency can be changed once established. Secondarily, Setter Injection can indicate that a dependency is not strictly required. You can then write your code without assuming that the dependency is present.
3. Combine the two when you want to have a dependency that is required but configurable.
4. Use Method Injection if you want to clearly indicate the means to alter a dependency.

5. Avoid Field Injection and prefer properties using Setter Injection.

That should provide you with a good overview of the basics of the different types of Dependency Injection. Once you have those principles down, you can make good use of the Spring Container.

12.4 The Delphi Spring Container and Service Locator

In the last chapter we got a very basic look at the Spring Container, using it to do all of our object creation and to push all of that creation back to the root of our application. In this section, we'll look a little more closely at the container: how to use it and what it can do, as well as the proper way to configure your application to take advantage of it.

The primary purpose of the container is to create objects. If you really want to follow the Single Responsibility Principle[1] in your classes, then it is not the job of a class to create its dependencies. Instead, a class should defer the responsibility of creation to a class that has the single responsibility of creating things. That's what a container is – a class whose single responsibility is to create things.

The primary purpose of the ServiceLocator is to retrieve implementations of requested services, whether they be implemented interfaces or just instances of objects. However, the techniques we'll see in this chapter will remove the need for the Service Locator, and by the end of the chapter I'll argue that its use is actually an anti-pattern.

The first thing you must do before using the container is to register the relevant classes. Here is a look at the Container's registration interface:

```
    function RegisterType<TComponentType>: TRegistration<TComponentType>; overloa\
d;
    function RegisterType(componentType: PTypeInfo): TRegistration; overload;
```

There are two ways to register a class: as a generic type or with the type information from the class. Thus, you can register a class in the following two ways:

```
    GlobalContainer.RegisterType<TSword>;
```

or

```
    GlobalContainer.RegisterType(TSword.ClassInfo);
```

---

[1]https://docs.google.com/file/d/0ByOwmqah_nuGNHEtcU5OekdDMkk/edit

I prefer using the generic method because it seems cleaner to me, but both ways will work.

One more note on registering classes – it is common practice to register your classes with the container in the initialization section of the unit where the class is implemented. That way, the registration takes place as close to the application root as possible. The weakness here is that the registration of your classes and interfaces takes place all over your application.

If you prefer to centralize your registrations, you can create a single unit that uses all the other units in your application, have that unit register all the classes and interfaces in a single method, and then call that single method at the very beginning of your program in the DPR file. The one thing to remember is that you also need to call GlobalContainer.Build to ensure that all the registrations take place and that the container can pull together all the information for the ServiceLocator to be able to do its job.

Registering Interfaces

Registering classes is great, but of course the real benefit comes when you register a particular class as implementing an interface. The call to RegisterType returns an instance of type TRegistration. TRegistration represents the result of registering a class and allows you to describe an interface that is implemented by the registered class. Thus, it has the following overloaded methods available for associating interfaces to classes:

```
function Implements(serviceType: PTypeInfo): TRegistration<T>; overload;
function Implements(serviceType: PTypeInfo; const name: string): TRegistratio\
n<T>; overload;
function Implements<TServiceType>: TRegistration<T>; overload;
function Implements<TServiceType>(const name: string): TRegistration<T>; over\
load;
```

Again, you can declare an implementing interface either by using generics or the type information for the interface. I'll be using the generics method throughout as I think it is easier to read and understand.

Note that two of the overloads here take a name parameter. I'll be discussing the benefits of this feature below.

Thus, you can now register TSword as implementing the IWeapon interface like so:

```
GlobalContainer.RegisterType<TSword>.Implements<IWeapon>;
```

Now the container will have an association between TSword and IWeapon that will allow it to create an instance of TWeapon when asked for an implemented reference of IWeapon. That might be done like so:

```
var
  Sword: IWeapon;
begin
  Sword := ServiceLocator.GetService<IWeapon>;
  Sword.Wield;
end;
```

Thus you can get a reference to TSword without having to create a reference to TSword or even putting TSword's unit name in your uses clause.

But looking at this, I see an immediate problem. We've registered a TSword against the IWeapon interface. But a knight uses more than a sword. What if he wants to use a mace or a lance? This is where registering interfaces by name comes in. The container allows you to register by name multiple classes against the same interface:

```
GlobalContainer.RegisterType<TSword>.Implements<IWeapon>('Sword');
GlobalContainer.RegisterType<TLance>.Implements<IWeapon>('Lance');
```

And now, if our knight wants to use a sword, we call:

```
var
  Sword: IWeapon;
begin
  Sword := ServiceLocator.GetService<IWeapon>('Sword');
  Sword.Wield;
end;
```

but if he needs to use his lance:

```
var
  Lance: IWeapon;
begin
  Lance := ServiceLocator.GetService<IWeapon>('Lance');
  Lance.Wield;
end;
```

You can register by name as many different implementations of a given interface as you like.

Lifetime Management

Since we are using interfaces, it is easy to forget about the lifetime of the objects behind those interfaces. As a consumer of interfaces, you don't normally worry about the lifetime of the implementing class because you know that it will be destroyed when the interface goes out of scope. However, things are a bit different when you are using the Container. Sometimes your implementing classes need finer lifetime control than just 'when the interface goes out of scope'. You may have limited resources associated with the class. You may want the same instance used for every request, or you may just want a new instance created for each request to the Container.

The Container lets you manage the lifetime of those objects by providing further methods on the `TRegistration` object that is returned when registering and declaring an implementation for a given class or interface.

`TRegistration` provides the following methods for determining the lifetime of the objects that it creates:

```
function AsSingleton: TRegistration; overload;
function AsSingleton(refCounting: TRefCounting): TRegistration; overload;
function AsSingletonPerThread: TRegistration;
function AsTransient: TRegistration;
function AsPooled(minPoolSize, maxPoolSize: Integer): TRegistration;
```

If you want to have your reference be a singleton – that is, one instance for all calls to the given registration – then declare it as follows:

```
GlobalContainer.RegisterType<TSword>.Implements<IWeapon>.AsSingleton;
```

That will ensure that whenever you ask for an `IWeapon`, you will be given back the same exact instance for all requests.

`AsSingletonPerThread` does what its name implies – it provides the same instance to each request within a given thread. There might be multiple instances of the implementation, but each thread will always get the same instance.

`AsTransient` is the default behavior. `AsTransient` will create a new instance for each request made. Assuming that you are using an interface reference, that transient instance will live as long as the interface remains in scope (i.e., as long as its reference count is greater than zero, presuming you are using "normal" reference counting).

`AsPooled` will create a pool of instances for use upon request. You can determine the minimum and maximum number of items in the pool. When an item is requested by the `ServiceLocator`, it will be retrieved from the pool of items. All the items in the pool are created when the container is built, and thus all are available when the program begins. Use pooling when creation is expensive and you want to pay that cost up front.

Custom Creation

As discussed, the main function of the Spring Container is to create objects for you. Normally it can do that because every object in Delphi has a default constructor or because the constructor's parameters are also registered in the Container. But what happens if your class has specific requirements for creation?

Well, the Spring Container provides for this via a method called DelegateTo, which allows you to provide an anonymous method that creates your object however you want to create it.

For instance, consider the following code:

```
type
  IWeapon = interface
    procedure Fire;
  end;

  TSword = class(TInterfacedObject, IWeapon)
  private
    FHasScope: Boolean;
  public
    constructor Create(aIsValerianSteel: Boolean);
  end;
```

You can register TSword with the container and grab it with the Service Locator, but it won't be properly instantiated because you don't have a way to get a hold of a sword with or without Valerian steel (In fact, because Boolean types always default to False, you'll always get a sword without Valerian steel.). What to do?

Well, here's what you do: You register two different instances by name, passing in an anonymous method that will create the sword as you want it to be created for each:

```
GlobalContainer.RegisterType<TSword>.Implements<IWeapon>('ValerianSteel')
  .DelegateTo(function: TSword
                begin
                  Result := TSword.Create(True);
                end);
GlobalContainer.RegisterType<TSword>.Implements<IWeapon>('RegularSteel')
  .DelegateTo(function: TSword
                begin
                  Result := TSword.Create(False);
                end);
```

Now we can grab from the container either a scoped or a non-scoped sword, thanks to the DelegateTo function and a simple anonymous function that returns an instance of TSword. Sweet.

Setting a Default Type

Since you can register multiple types to the same interface by name, it's possible to create an ambiguous situation when asking for an implementation without a name. Consider the following:

Say you register two weapons by name:

```
initialization
    GlobalContainer.RegisterType<TSword>.Implements<IWeapon>('sword');
    GlobalContainer.RegisterType<TDagger>.Implements<IWeapon>('dagger');
```

... but then later, you ask for a weapon without a name attached.

```
var
  Dagger: IWeapon;
begin
    Dagger := ServiceLocator.GetService<IWeapon>;
end;
```

If you do this, you'll get an "Unsatisfied Dependency" exception, because the container doesn't know which weapon you want. And of course, you won't know this until runtime. Alas.

But there is a solution. You can declare one of the weapons as the default weapon, and it will be the one returned if there is any ambiguity about which IWeapon is required. Thus, you should declare your registrations as follows:

```
initialization
    GlobalContainer.RegisterType<TSword>.Implements<IWeapon>('sword');
    GlobalContainer.RegisterType<TDagger>.Implements<IWeapon>('dagger').AsDefault<\
IWeapon>;
```

Thus, if you ask for an IWeapon without a name, you'll get the dagger by default. Note, though, that if you ask for an IWeapon with a name that doesn't exist, you'll still get an exception and not the default weapon.

Register the same type for two interfaces

Sometimes a class can implement more than one interface. Well, no problem – you can register that class as implementing both of those interfaces in a single, chained together statement:

```
  TSharpEdgedShield = class(TInterfacedObject, IWeapon, IShield)
    procedure WieldWeapon;
    procedure Block;
  end;


  GlobalContainer.RegisterType<TSharpEdgedShield>.Implements<IWeapon>('shield')
                                      .Implements<IShield>('sharpshiel\
d');
```

Using Registration to Inject Fields and Properties

Many times, you'll have one registered class that has a field or property of a type that is also a registered class. When this happens, you can use the container to automatically connect up the field or property with the appropriate, registered implementation. This means that you don't actually have to create or even assign instances for your fields and properties; the container will do it for you instead 'auto-magically'.

For instance, consider this set of types:

```
type
  IFirearm = interface
  ['{47C93F4A-D07F-4E66-964C-6E21A3F4AB17}']
    procedure Fire;
  end;


  IAimingDevice = interface
  ['{3DB34251-B82B-443D-AF1C-7182DC46D014}']
    procedure Aim;
  end;

  TScope = class(TInterfacedObject, IAimingDevice)
    procedure Aim;
  end;

  TRifle = class(TInterfacedObject, IFirearm)
  private
    FScope: IAimingDevice;
  public
    procedure Fire;
    property Scope: IAimingDevice read FScope write FScope;
  end;
```

Here we have a TRifle class that has a Scope interface property of type IAimingDevice. TScope is an implementation of IAimingDevice. Thus, we can register all of these classes like so:

```
GlobalContainer.RegisterType<TRifle>.Implements<IFirearm>.InjectProperty('Scope\
');
  GlobalContainer.RegisterType<TScope>.Implements<IAimingDevice>;
```

The first registration means "Register the type TRifle as implementing the interface IWeapon, and when you see the property named Scope, go ahead and grab an implementation of that class from the container based on its type."

The next line registers TScope as the implementer for the IAimingDevice interface, thus completing the loop. Because TScope is of type IAimingDevice and because TScope is registered as implementing IAimingDevice, everything gets all hooked up just fine. This is just another easier step in 'wiring together' your classes. It also allows you to pass off the creation of objects to the Container.

The same basic principle works for fields:

```
TRifle = class(TInterfacedObject, IFirearm)
private
  FScope: IAimingDevice;
  FMetalSight: IAimingDevice;
public
  Clip: IClip;
  procedure Fire;
  property Scope: IAimingDevice read FScope write FScope;
  property MetalSight: IAimingDevice read FMetalSight write FMetalSight;
end;
```

```
GlobalContainer.RegisterType<TRifle>.Implements<IFirearm>.InjectProperty('Metal\
Sight', 'sight')
                                                .InjectField('Clip');
  GlobalContainer.RegisterType<TScope>.Implements<IAimingDevice>('scope').AsDefau\
lt<IAimingDevice>;
  GlobalContainer.RegisterType<TNormalSight>.Implements<IAimingDevice>('sight');
  GlobalContainer.RegisterType<T14RoundClip>.Implements<IClip>;
```

Since we register T14RoundClip as implementing IClip, we can inject the field named Clip with an instance of T14RoundClip because it implements IClip.

This all works, of course, because everything is registered with the same container. The container knows about all the types involved. It can use RTTI to create any type registered within it. When it comes time to create an instance of a given implementation, the container can iterate over all of the fields and properties, and if any of them have registered "injections", then those types can be instantiated an assigned as well. Thus, through a combination of the power of generics and the 'magic' of RTTI, the DI container can provide a lot of power. In a bit, we'll see how we can even label fields and properties with attributes in order to ensure that they are automatically 'wired up' for you.

Using Registration to Inject Constructors and Methods

When you register a class/interface pair in the container, it can inject an instance for you anywhere that interface is found. So far, we've been using Constructor Injection to pass in dependencies to a class. That is, we've used the parameters of a class's constructor to pass in to it the dependencies it needs to do its job. Then, in the implementation of the constructor, instead of creating an instance of the dependency, we've retrieved it from the container. This works really nicely because it couples you only to the interfaces that you have in the constructors of your objects.

But that whole process seems rather algorithmic, right? And you know that RTTI can tell you everything about the parameters of the constructor, right? Doesn't it stand to reason that this process could happen in an automated way? Of course it does.

The Container can actually inject an entire constructor into your class so that you use that class without actually having to manually call the Service Locator. This is commonly referred to as "auto-wiring."

Code always explains things well. Let's return to our Knight and give him an interface.

```
IFightable = interface
['{A24A33AD-ADD5-442A-A909-1BF7D3FE0237}']
  procedure Fight;
end;


TKnight = class(TInterfacedObject, IFightable)
private
  FWeapon: IWeapon;
public
  constructor Create(aWeapon: IWeapon);
  procedure Fight;
end;


constructor TKnight.Create(aWeapon: IWeapon);
begin
  inherited Create;
  FWeapon := aWeapon;
end;


procedure TKnight.Fight;
begin
  Write('The Knight engages in battle! ');
  FWeapon.WieldWeapon;
end;
```

. . .

```
   GlobalContainer.RegisterType<TSword>.Implements<IWeapon>('sword').AsDefault<IWe\
apon>;
   GlobalContainer.RegisterType<TDagger>.Implements<IWeapon>('dagger');

   GlobalContainer.RegisterType<TKnight>.Implements<IFightable>.InjectConstructor(\
['sword']);
```

As you can see, TKnight's constructor takes an IWeapon. Well, given the above registrations, the container knows about Knights, swords, daggers, and fighting. The last registration also contains something new – a call to InjectConstructor. It takes as its last parameter a string naming one of the IWeapon registrations, in this case the 'sword'. Given all of that information, the container can now "inject" an IWeapon into the constructor of TKnight when it is called internally. Because the parameter is a type registered in the Container, the system can look up the implementing type by name ('sword') and create a sword for use in the constructor. So now, the following code works just fine:

```
procedure KnightFights;
var
  Knight: IFightable;
begin
  Knight := ServiceLocator.GetService<IFightable>;
  Knight.Fight;
end;
```

The thing to note is that nowhere in your code does an instance for IWeapon get created or even retrieved via the ServiceLocator. The Container knows that you've told it the way to construct a TKnight and properly injects a sword into the constructor when it creates an instance of TKnight for the IFightable interface.

But what if you need to pass in more than just registered types? Constructors don't always cooperate and take only registered types, right? Well, you can do that, too.

Let's create a new class, TKing, where the constructor takes a string parameter that gives the king a name in addition to the Weapon that every good king should have.

```
TKing = class
private
  FWeapon: IWeapon;
  FName: string;
public
  constructor Create(aWeapon: IWeapon; aName: string);
  procedure Fight;
end;
```

The `InjectConstructor` method can take an `array of TValue` as a parameter, allowing you to register all the parameters of the constructor for `TKing`:

```
GlobalContainer.RegisterType<TKing>.InjectConstructor(['sword', 'Arthur']);
```

In this case, we have given the king the name "Arthur" and a sword for a weapon (Remember, registered items are retrieved by name and thus must be registered by name.).

12.5 Registering via attributes

Back in the attributes chapter, we saw how you can use brackets ([]) to declare attributes to add your own runtime information to classes.

The Spring Container provides attributes to mark constructors, fields, properties, and methods as injected. By using the `[Inject]` attribute, you can mark a class member as requiring the container to inject a value for it, and avoid registering it explicitly. In general, an attribute is clearer code because the declaration is right next to the affected class member, rather than separated off in a registration call in an `initialization` section.

The `[Inject]` attribute can be used to replace any of the method registration calls that we discussed in the previous section. You can place the `[Inject]` attribute on fields, properties, and the parameters of methods and constructors. The attribute can also take a string parameter that will correspond to the name of the item that should be injected.

Let's look at a code example. This example will show the `[Inject]` attribute attached to a field, a property, and the parameter of a constructor.

First, here are some interfaces:

```
type
  IFireFighter = interface
  ['{12188A33-536C-483E-A0C7-D372EDDF63B1}']
    procedure FightFire;
  end;

  IFireTool = interface
  ['{D70EACE6-9F78-43AE-AFB1-2AE20FE117B2}']
    procedure UseToFightFire;
  end;
```

The first is an interface to describe anyone that fights a fire. IFireTool is designed to represent anything that an IFireFighter would use to fight a fire.

Next, we'll implement these interfaces:

```
TFireHose = class(TInterfacedObject, IFireTool)
  procedure UseToFightFire;
end;

TAxe = class(TInterfacedObject, IFireTool)
  procedure UseToFightFire;
end;

TProtectiveGear = class(TInterfacedObject, IFireTool)
  procedure UseToFightFire;
end;

TFireman = class(TInterfacedObject, IFireFighter)
private
  [Inject('gear')]
  FGear: IFireTool;
  FMainTool: IFireTool;
  FSecondaryTool: IFireTool;
public
  constructor Create([Inject('hose')]aTool: IFireTool);
  [Inject('axe')]
  property SecondaryTool: IFireTool read FSecondaryTool write FSecondaryTool;
  procedure FightFire;
end;
```

and here's the registration:

```
initialization
  GlobalContainer.RegisterType<TFireman>.Implements<IFireFighter>;
  GlobalContainer.RegisterType<TFireHose>.Implements<IFireTool>('hose');
  GlobalContainer.RegisterType<TAxe>.Implements<IFireTool>('axe');
  GlobalContainer.RegisterType<TProtectiveGear>.Implements<IFireTool>('gear');
```

The first thing to note is that the registrations are simplified: There is no call to `InjectConstructor`, `InjectField`, or `InjectProperty`. Second, I've left the implementations out to keep things concise, but they are exactly what you'd expect: nothing but assignments and calls to `WriteLn`. What is most noticeably missing is any call to `Create`. Everything is injected, either via property or constructor injection.

The key part to note here is the three uses of the `[Inject]` attribute. The first is on the field `FGear`, which tells the container "When you need to create an instance of `TFireman`, grab the implementation of `IFireTool` named 'gear' and assign it to `FGear`. The second is basically the same thing for the `SecondaryTool` property, and the third is for the parameter of type `IFireTool` on the constructor of `TFireman`. All three basically inform the container what to create and assign when the `TFireman` class is created. There's no need for you to create anything, and there's no need to have any kind of hard-coded coupling to any particular implementation.

This is a simple, contrived demo. In a real application, you should put your interfaces into a separate unit, and then use only that unit when dealing with the functionality they provide. Implementations should be referred to only in the DPR file with their registrations taking place in implementation sections.

Some general things to note:

- Method Injection and Constructor Injection are unfortunate names. They both tend to give you the idea that you are adding in a method or a constructor to your class. Better terms might have been "Injection via Constructor" and "Injection via Method".
- You can have a lot of control over what implementations get injected. Since you can register a class/interface pair by name and then inject them by name, you can configure your application in different ways based on those names.
- Because attributes are simple to deploy, direct replacements for registration calls, and easier to see in code, I recommend that you use them as much as possible as opposed to direct registration calls.
- The one downside here is that the use of attributes does tie you to the specific implementation in the Spring Framework. Using `[Inject]` is specific to the Spring Framework. By using the registration methods, you could theoretically replace the `IContainer` interface with a different implementation. Using the `[Inject]` attribute means you are tied to the Spring Framework more closely.

12.6 `ServiceLocator` as Anti-pattern

An "anti-pattern" is defined as "a pattern used in ... software engineering that may be commonly used but is ineffective and/or counterproductive in practice[2]." Anti-patterns should be avoided, yet sometimes they appear to be good or proper solutions to problems.

In all of the examples so far, we have relied on multiple calls to `ServiceLocator`. They have occurred as far back as they can – at the point when there is no more constructor injection to be done. In the next section, though, I'm going to argue that `ServiceLocator` is an anti-pattern and shouldn't be used except once at the very root of your program.

So in the previous demos, we used the ServiceLocator to grab instances of registered classes. It helped us to properly decouple the code and end up with nothing but a unit of interfaces in your uses clause. Nice. Things were really well decoupled. However, those calls might start to bug you after a while – they did me. I noticed that, in essence, the calls to `ServiceLocator` merely became replacements for calls to `Create`. They became a proxy for the very code that we were trying to avoid.

Now here is the thing: you can write all of that code without using the `ServiceLocator`, and instead, you can accomplish the same thing by injecting everything. Previously, we used these methods to inject dependencies:

```
function InjectConstructor(const parameterTypes: array of PTypeInfo): TRegistrati\
on<T>; overload;
function InjectProperty(const propertyName: string): TRegistration<T>; overload;
function InjectMethod(const methodName: string): TRegistration<T>; overload;
function InjectMethod(const methodName: string; const parameterTypes: array of PT\
ypeInfo): TRegistration<T>; overload;
function InjectField(const fieldName: string): TRegistration<T>; overload;
```

These methods allow you to inject (duh) different items into your classes and automatically instantiate them as a result. And when you inject something directly with them, the Container becomes smart enough to create them for you automatically, even without the psuedo-Create call that is `ServiceLocator`.

We've discussed how you should be using Constructor Injection (and possibly Setter Injection) as often as you can, and how you need to push the creation of your component graph all the way back to the composite root. In Delphi, that means all the way back to the first line of the DPR file. And if you do that, you could end up with this monster constructor that requires every single class your application needs. Think about it – every class dependency, with its constructors passing in dependencies for its dependencies, and so on, and you could end up with a royal mess back at the very root of the problem.

But remember, every time you use one of the five above methods, you eliminate the need for a call to the `ServiceLocator`. Thus, it stands to reason that they can be used to cause the creation of

---

[2]http://en.wikipedia.org/wiki/Anti-pattern

every single class needed for your application during the registration process. They can completely eliminate the need for you to ever call the ServiceLocator (with one exception, discussed below) because if you can call the ServiceLocator, you can use these methods to register the connection between what you need the ServiceLocator for and the registration process.

Put another way, every call to the ServiceLocator can be replaced by a registration call. You don't need the ServiceLocator because the registration process alone is enough.

Consider the following unit of code:

```
unit uNoServiceLocatorDemo;

interface

uses
      Spring.Container
    , Spring.Services
    , Spring.Collections
    ;

type
  IWeapon = interface
  ['{0F63DF32-F65F-4708-958E-E1931814EC33}']
    procedure Weild;
  end;

  IFighter = interface
  ['{0C926753-A70D-40E3-8C35-85CA2C4B18CA}']
    procedure Fight;
  end;

  TBattleField = class
  private
    FFighter: IFighter;
  public
    procedure AddFighter(aFighter: IFighter);
    procedure Battle;
  end;

  TSword = class(TInterfacedObject, IWeapon)
    procedure Weild;
  end;

  TKnight = class(TInterfacedObject, IFighter)
```

```
  private
    FWeapon: IWeapon;
  public
    constructor Create(aWeapon: IWeapon);
    procedure Fight;
  end;

implementation

procedure TBattleField.AddFighter(aFighter: IFighter);
begin
  FFighter := aFighter;
end;

procedure TBattleField.Battle;
begin
  WriteLn('The Battle is on!');
  FFighter.Fight;
end;

constructor TKnight.Create(aWeapon: IWeapon);
begin
  inherited Create;
  FWeapon := aWeapon;
end;

procedure TKnight.Fight;
begin
  WriteLn('The knight swings into action!');
  FWeapon.Weild;
end;

procedure TSword.Weild;
begin
  WriteLn('"Swoosh" goes the sword!');
end;

initialization

  GlobalContainer.RegisterType<TSword>.Implements<IWeapon>('sword');
  GlobalContainer.RegisterType<TKnight>.Implements<IFighter>('knight');
```

```
end.
```

Here we have some classes that are all nicely decoupled. Our registrations are neatly named. The classes use constructor injection to ask for their dependencies, and the TKnight and the TSword are nicely registered, just waiting to be grabbed and used in a decoupled way using the ServiceLocator. All is great. And then, in order to actually have our cast of characters do anything, you might do something like this:

```
procedure FightBattle;
var
  Battlefield: TBattleField;
  TempKnight: IFighter;
  TempSword: IWeapon;
begin
  Battlefield := TBattleField.Create;
  try
    TempKnight := ServiceLocator.GetService<IFighter>;
    TempSword := ServiceLocator.GetService<IWeapon>;
    TempKnight.Weapon := TempSword;
    Battlefield.AddFighter(TempKnight);
    Battlefield.Battle;
  finally
    Battlefield.Free;
  end;
end;
```

You need a knight and a sword? Well, just call the ServiceLocator, grab the sword, arm the knight, add him to the battle, and off it goes.

It all works, and it is all decoupled. But you are still using the ServiceLocator as a replacement for calls to Create. Again, that's cool – things are decoupled, but...

The argument against the ServiceLocator is pretty simple: It's a singleton, singletons are global variables, and global variables are bad. Plus, if you don't need it, why use it?

Well, you don't need it. Watch.

The rule of thumb is that you get one call to the ServiceLocator at the very root of your application. You get one shot. We'll see that one shot below.

Let's change how we register our classes and interfaces:

```
GlobalContainer.RegisterType<TBattleField>.InjectMethod('AddFighter', ['knight']);

GlobalContainer.RegisterType<TSword>.Implements<IWeapon>('sword');
GlobalContainer.RegisterType<TKnight>.Implements<IFighter>('knight').InjectConstr\
uctor(['sword']);
```

Some things to note:

- We only changed the way things were registered. We didn't change the class structure or relationships at all.
- We are now registering TBattlefield. We need to do that for two reasons. First, it is the "root" of the application for our simple example. It is the place where everything starts in relation to our object graph. To get an instance of TBattlefield, we make our one allowable call to ServiceLocator. Second, we need to inject a method, as discussed next.
- Into TBattleField we have injected a method, specifically the AddFighter method. Here's what the call to InjectMethod does – it says "When the container creates an instance of TBattlefield, look up the AddFighter method and pass to it as its parameter an instance of the interface named 'knight'." Thus, when the container creates an instance of TBattleField for you, the AddFighter method will be automatically called, and a valid weapon will be passed to it. There goes one call to the ServiceLocator.
- The second call to ServiceLocator is eliminated by the call to InjectConstructor. This registration now means "When you ask for an IFighter, create an instance of TKnight, and when you do, pass the constructor an IWeapon from the registered type named 'sword'." Again, there goes the other call to ServiceLocator.
- Thus we've used the container to "wire up" all the dependencies and ensure that they are properly created before the main class or any other class is even asked for. The call to GlobalContainer.Build in the DPR file will ensure this takes place.

Finally, we run everything with the much simpler and cleaner:

```
procedure FightBattle;
var
  Battlefield: TBattleField;
begin
  Battlefield := ServiceLocator.GetService<TBattlefield>;
  try
    Battlefield.Battle;
  finally
    Battlefield.Free;
  end;
end;
```

And there's our one call to ServiceLocator at the very root of our application (FightBattle gets called in the DPR file as this is a console application).

You can do the same thing with constructors – you can call InjectConstructor, passing the names of registrations for each of the parameters in the constructor. And if need be, for both InjectConstructor and InjectMethod, you can add in non-registered parameters such as integers and strings, etc.

Bottom line: Use the injection methods and the container to connect up your classes and inject dependencies, not the ServiceLocator.

12.7 Dependency Injection Summary

Do's.

1. Do program against interfaces, not implementations.
2. Do keep constructors simple – assignments only and no logic.
3. Do use constructor injection everywhere you can.
4. Do use a container to do all your creating.
5. Do give a name to all your implementation registrations.
6. Do use injection methods and attributes to hook up all your dependencies.

Dont's:

1. Don't mix UI code and business logic
2. Don't use event handlers for anything other than displaying data and changing the UI. Don't put business logic in your UI event handlers.
3. Don't create anything except known, proven RTL classes and the like.
4. Don't use the Service Locator anywhere except at the very root of your application.

[1] http://en.wikipedia.org/wiki/Anti-pattern

13 Unit Testing

Am I suggesting 100% test coverage? No, I'm demanding it. Every single line of code that you write should be tested. Period.

I don't want management to mandate 100% test coverage. I want your conscience to mandate it as a point of honor.

How about: if you have 100%, you can refactor savagely whenever you want with confidence.

I took the above quotes from a Twitter conversation that Uncle Bob Martin[1] had with some of his followers. He is pretty passionate about code coverage and unit testing. We all might not be quite as serious as Uncle Bob, but we all definitely should be at least a little passionate about unit testing.

And that passion should stem from a desire to write good code. I'm going to make the case that the only way you can call your code "good" is if it is fully unit tested. If you write and deliver code that isn't completely unit tested, you should feel like you are walking down the street naked. You should feel exposed and like everyone is looking at you. You should believe firmly that your code will fail miserably unless it is completely covered by unit tests.

13.1 So What is Unit Testing?

Unit testing is the testing of code to ensure that it performs the task that it is meant to perform. It tests code at the very lowest level possible – the individual methods of your classes. It is the key to writing clean, maintainable code. If you concentrate on writing code that is easily testable, you can't help but end up with decoupled, clean, high-quality code that is easy to maintain. What's not to like?

But sometimes there are questions over the definition of terms when it comes to unit testing. For instance, what, exactly, is a "unit"? What does "mocking" mean? How do I know whether I actually am doing unit testing? In this chapter, we'll cover what these terms all mean, and then we'll take a look at a simple example that illustrates the way to go about writing tests and code together.

---

[1] https://twitter.com/unclebobmartin

What is a "Unit"?

The first question that comes up when discussing unit testing is, well, what is a unit? You can't do unit testing without knowing what a unit is.

When it comes to unit testing, I view a "unit" as any discreet module of code that can be tested in isolation. It can be something as simple as a stand-alone routine (think `StringReplace` or `IncMonth`), but normally it will be a single class and its methods. A class is the basic, discrete code entity of modern languages. In Delphi, classes (and records which are conceptually very similar) are the base building blocks of your code. They are the data structures that, when used together, form a system.

In the world of unit testing, that class is generally referred to as the "Class Under Test (CUT)" or the "System Under Test (SUT)." You'll see those terms used extensively – to the point where it is strongly recommended that you use CUT as the variable name for your classes being tested.

> **Definition**: A unit is any code entity that can be tested in isolation, usually a class.

Am I Actually Doing Unit Testing?

So when you are doing unit testing, you are generally testing classes (And for the sake of the discussion, that will be the assumption hereafter.). But the key thing to note is that when unit testing a class, you are unit testing the given class and only the given class. Unit testing is always done in isolation – that is, the class under test needs to be completely isolated from any other classes or any other systems. If you are testing a class and you need some external entity, then you are no longer unit testing. A class is only "testable" when it's dependencies can be and are "faked" and thus tested without any of its real external dependencies. So if you are running what you think is a unit test, and that test needs to access a database, a file system, or any other external system, then you have stopped doing unit testing and you've started doing integration testing.

One thing I want to be clear about: There's no shame in doing integration testing. Integration testing is really important and should be done. Unit testing frameworks are often a very good way to do integration testing. I don't want to leave you with the impression that because integration is not unit testing, you shouldn't be doing it – quite the contrary. Nevertheless, it is an important distinction. The point here is to recognize what unit tests are and to strive to write them when it is intended to write them. By all means, write integration tests, but don't write them in lieu of unit testing.

Think of it this way: Every unit test framework – DUnit and DUnitX included – creates a test executable. If you can't take that test executable and run it successfully on your mother's computer in a directory that is read only, then you aren't unit testing anymore.

> **Definition**: Unit testing is the act of testing a single class in isolation, completely apart from any of its actual dependencies.

> **Definition**: Integration testing is the act of testing a single class along with one or more of its actual external dependencies.

What is an Isolation Framework?

Commonly, developers have used the term "mocking framework" to describe code that provides faking services to allow classes to be tested in isolation. However, as we'll see below (and discuss more fully in the next chapter), a "mock" is actually a specific kind of fake class, along with stubs. Thus, it is probably more accurate to use the term "Isolation Framework" instead of "Mocking Framework." A good isolation framework will allow for the easy creation of both types of fakes – mocks and stubs.

Fakes allow you to test a class in isolation by providing implementations of dependencies without requiring the real dependencies.

> **Definition**: An isolation framework is a collection of code that enables the easy creation of fakes.

> **Definition**: A Fake Class is any class that provides functionality sufficient to pretend that it is a dependency needed by a class under test. There are two kind of fakes – stubs and mocks.

If you really want to learn about this stuff in depth, I strongly recommend you read "The Art of Unit Testing: With Examples in .Net" by Roy Osherove[2]. For you Delphi guys, don't be scared off by the C# examples – this book is a great treatise on unit testing and gives plenty of descriptions, proper techniques, and definitions of unit testing in far more detail than I've done here. Or you can listen to Roy talk to Scott Hanselman on the Hanselminutes podcast[3]. If you really want to get super geeky, get a hold of a copy of "xUnit Test Patterns: Refactoring Test Code" by Gerard Meszaros[4]. This heavy tome is a tour de force of unit testing, outlining a complete taxonomy of tests and testing patterns. It's not for the faint of heart, but if you read that book, you'll know everything there is to know and then some.

Stubs

A stub is a class that does the absolute minimum to appear to be an actual dependency for the Class Under Test. It provides no functionality required by the test, except to appear to implement a given interface or descend from a given base class. When the CUT calls it, a stub usually does nothing. Stubs are completely peripheral to testing the CUT, and exist purely to enable the CUT to run. A typical example is a stub that provides logging services. The CUT may need an implementation of, say, ILogger in order to execute, but none of the tests care about the logging. In fact, you specifically don't want the CUT logging anything. Thus, the stub pretends to be the logging service

---

[2]http://www.amazon.com/gp/product/1617290890/ref=as_li_ss_tl?ie=UTF8&camp=1789&creative=390957&creativeASIN=1617290890&linkCode=as2&tag=nickhodgeshomepa

[3]http://hanselminutes.com/169/the-art-of-unit-testing-with-roy-osherove

[4]http://www.amazon.com/gp/product/0131495054/ref=as_li_ss_tl?ie=UTF8&camp=1789&creative=390957&creativeASIN=0131495054&linkCode=as2&tag=nickhodgeshomepa

by implementing the interface, but that implementation actually does nothing. Its implementing methods might literally be empty. Furthermore, while a stub might return data for the purpose of keeping the CUT happy and running, it can never take any action that will fail a test. If it does, then it ceases to be a stub, and it becomes a "mock."

> **Definition**: A stub is a fake that has no effect on the passing or failing of the test and that exists purely to allow the test to run.

Mocks

Mocks are a bit more complicated. Mocks do what stubs do in that they provide a fake implementation of a dependency needed by the CUT. However, they go beyond being a mere stub by recording the interaction between itself and the CUT. A mock keeps a record of all the interactions with the CUT and reports back, passing the test if the CUT behaved correctly, and failing the test if it did not. Thus, it is actually the Mock, and not the CUT itself, that determines if a test passes or fails.

Here is an example – say you have a class `TWidgetProcessor`. It has two dependencies, an `ILogger` and an `IVerifier`. In order to test `TWidgetProcessor`, you need to fake both of those dependencies. However, in order to really test `TWidgetProcessor`, you'll want to do two tests - one where you stub `ILogger` and test the interaction with `IVerifier`, and another where you stub `IVerifier` and test the interaction with `ILogger`. Both require fakes, but in each case, you'll provide a stub class for one and a mock class for the other.

Let's look a bit closer at the first scenario – where we stub out `ILogger` and use a mock for `IVerifier`. The stub we've discussed – you either write an empty implementation of `ILogger`, or you use an isolation framework to implement the interface to do nothing. However, the fake for `IVerifier` becomes a bit more interesting – it needs a mock class. Say the process of verifying a widget takes two steps: first the processor needs to see if the widget is in the system, and then, if it is, the processor needs to check if the widget is properly configured.

Thus, if you are testing the `TWidgetProcessor`, you need to run a test that checks whether `TWidgetProcessor` makes the second call if it gets `True` back from the first call. This test will require the mock class to do two things: first, it needs to return `True` from the first call, and then it needs to keep track of whether or not the resulting configuration call actually gets made. Then it becomes the job of the mock class to provide the pass/fail information – if the second call is made after the first call returns `True`, then the test passes; if not, the test fails. This is what makes this fake class a mock: The mock itself contains the information that needs to be checked for the pass/fail criteria.

> **Definition**: A mock is a fake that keeps track of the behavior of the Class Under Test and passes or fails the test based on that behavior.

Most isolation frameworks include the ability to do extensive and sophisticated tracking of exactly what happens inside a mock class. For instance, mocks can not only tell if a given method was called, it can track the number of times given methods are called and the parameters that are passed to those calls. They can determine and decide if something is called that isn't supposed to be, or if something isn't called that is supposed to be. As part of the test setup, you can tell the mock exactly what to expect, and to fail if that exact sequence of events and parameters is not executed as expected. Stubs are fairly easy and straightforward, but mocks can get rather sophisticated.

In the next chapter, we'll take a closer look at the Delphi Mocks Framework[5]. It takes advantage of some cool new RTL features that first appeared in Delphi XE2. It's also a very generous and awesome gift to the Delphi community from Vince Parrett, who makes the very awesome FinalBuilder[6]. If you have XE2 or newer and are doing unit testing, you should get Delphi Mocks and use it. If you don't have XE2 or above and are doing unit testing, you should upgrade so you can start using this very valuable isolation framework.

But again, the whole point here is to test your classes in isolation; you want your CUT to be able to perform its duties without any outside, real, external dependencies.

Thus, a final definition:

> Unit testing is the testing of a single code entity when isolated completely from its dependencies.

13.2 Why Do Unit Testing?

I find that there is a lot of resistance to doing unit testing. Many developers seem to view it as a waste of time or as effort that will merely delay the completion of a project under deadline. They feel that they can't get any benefit from it. I couldn't disagree more. Here's why.

Unit Testing will find bugs

Whether you do Test Driven Development and write your tests first, write your tests as you go along, or write tests long after the code as been written, unit testing will find bugs. When you write a full suite of tests that define what the expected behavior is for a given class, anything in that class that isn't behaving as expected will be revealed.

Unit Testing will keep bugs away

A complete and thorough suite of unit tests will help to ensure that any bugs that creep into your code will be revealed immediately. Make a change that introduces a bug, and your tests can reveal it the very next time you run your tests. If you find a bug that is outside the realm of your unit test suite and you can write a test for it to ensure that the bug never returns.

---

[5]https://github.com/VSoftTechnologies/Delphi-Mocks
[6]http://www.finalbuilder.com

Unit Testing saves time

This is the most controversial notion about unit testing. Most developers believe that writing unit tests takes more time than it saves. I don't believe this - in fact, I argue the opposite. Writing unit tests helps ensure that your code is working as designed right from the start. Unit tests define what your code should do, and thus you won't spend time writing code that does things that it shouldn't do. Every unit test becomes a regression test, ensuring that things continue to work as designed while you develop. They help ensure that subsequent changes don't break things. They help ensure that what you write the first time is the right thing. All of these benefits save time both in the short and the long term.

And if you think about it, you already test your code while you are writing it. Maybe you write a simple console app. At the very least you compile and see it running. No one checks in code that they don't believe works, and you have to do *something* to make yourself think that it works. Spend that time writing unit tests, and you'll have decoupled working coding with a suite of regression tests.

Unit Testing gives peace of mind

Having a full, complete, and thorough set of tests that cover the complete functionality of your code might be difficult to achieve, but having it will give you peace of mind. You can run all those tests and know that your code works as it is supposed to. You can refactor and change the code knowing that if you break anything, you'll know right away. Knowing the state of your code, that it works, and that you can update and improve it without fear is a very good thing.

All code ages, but you can keep your code from ever truly becoming legacy code. There are a number of ways to define legacy code, but one way is "Code you are afraid to touch". If your code has unit tests, it is really hard for it to become legacy code. Many of us have that chunk of code that we are afraid to touch – but with unit testing, you'll not have that kind of code. Unit testing removes that fear of touching code. In "Working Effectively with Legacy Code[7]," Michael Feathers goes so far as to define legacy code as any code that doesn't have unit tests. Want to avoid your code becoming legacy code? Write unit tests for it.

Unit Testing documents the proper use of a class

One of the benefits of unit testing is that your tests can define for subsequent developers how the class should be used. Unit tests become, in effect, simple examples of how your code works, what it is expected to do, and the proper way to use the code being tested. Consumers of your code can look to your unit tests for information about the proper way to make your code do what it is supposed to do.

---

[7]http://www.amazon.com/gp/product/0131177052/ref=as_li_ss_tl?ie=UTF8&camp=1789&creative=390957&creativeASIN=0131177052&linkCode=as2&tag=nickhodgeshomepa"

13.3 Unit Testing in Delphi

For many years, the main unit testing framework has been DUnit[8]. Based on the original Delphi RTTI, it's been the mainstay of Delphi unit testing for a decade or more. DUnit is a complete xUnit testing solution, but while venerable and well-used, it is at this point somewhat outdated.

Recently a new framework has appeared called DUnitX[9]. DUnitX leverages attributes and Delphi's new RTTI to make test classes and methods more flexible and easy to manage. As of this writing, DUnitX is quite usable but still under development.

I'll be discussing both here in the book. First, I'll give a basic overview of each and how they work, and then I'll be mixing in examples of each as we go along.

DUnit

DUnit was originally published in the late 1990s and was written by Juanco Añez. He followed the original pattern set forth for all xUnit frameworks defined by Kent Beck[10]. DUnit is an open source project that can be found on SourceForge. [11]

Starting with Delphi 2005, DUnit has shipped with RAD Studio and has been integrated into the IDE. Developers can use the IDE expert to automatically generate test cases for a given Delphi unit.

DUnit is based on the "old" RTTI built into Delphi. Tests are based on a class called `TTestCase`. To use `TTestCase`, you create a descendant class and add published methods as tests. The framework then uses RTTI to find all the published methods and execute them.

Testing is done using a set of overloaded functions that start with `CheckXXX`, such as `CheckEquals` or `CheckNotEquals`. They take as parameters an expected value, an actual value, and an optional message parameter that lets you provide information for output in the event of a test failure. The `Check` calls raise an internal exception if the test fails, and in this way tests can be tracked as passing or failing. `TTestCase` also included virtual methods called `Setup` and `TearDown` that allow you to do as their names say – setup things for testing and then "tear down" anything you created in `Setup`. `Setup` and `TearDown` are run once for every test, allowing you to ensure that each test is run with a "clean slate."

DUnitX

DUnitX, on the other hand, utilized the new RTTI to allow any class you want to contain tests. Using the [TestFixture] attribute on a class allows it to contain methods that are tests. Any method on such a class can be labeled as a test by attaching the attribute [Test] to it. Setup and tear down is done by decorating any method with [Setup] and [TearDown] attributes. In addition, the framework

---

[8]http://dunit.sourceforge.net/

[9]https://github.com/VSoftTechnologies/DUnitX

[10]http://en.wikipedia.org/wiki/Kent_Beck

[11]http://dunit.sourceforge.net/

allows for test fixture level setup and tear down with the [SetupFixture] and [TearDownFixture] attributes. These last two are called once per test run. DUnitX is also an open source project that can be found on GitHub[12].

As I said, as of this writing, DUnitX is still in development. It can be used to create Console applications for visual output. In addition, you can integrated it into your continuous integration solution by using the XML output. A graphical output is currently in the works.

13.4 General Rules for Unit Tests

Test one thing at a time in isolation.

This is probably the baseline rule to follow when it comes to unit tests. All classes should be tested in isolation. They should not depend on anything other than mocks and stubs. They shouldn't depend on the results of other tests. They should be able to run on any machine. You should be able to take your unit test executable and run it on your mother's machine while it isn't even connected to the Internet.

Follow the AAA rule: Arrange, Act, Assert

When it comes to unit testing, AAA stands for "Arrange, Act, Assert". It is a general pattern for writing individual tests to make them more readable and effective. First, you "Arrange." In this step, you set things up to be tested. You set variables, fields and properties to enable the test to be run, as well as define the expected result. Then you "Act" – that is, you actually call the method that you are testing. Finally, you "Assert" – call the testing framework to verify that the result of your "Act" is what was expected. Follow the AAA principle, and your test will be clear and easy to read.

Here's an example of a test that follows the AAA rule:

```
procedure TDateUtilsOfTests.TestDateOf;
var
  Expected: TDateTime;
  Actual: TDateTime;
  Input: TDateTime;
begin
  //Arrange
  Input := EncodeDateTime(1944, 1, 2, 3, 4, 5, 6);
  Expected := EncodeDate(1944, 1, 2);
  //Act
  Actual := DateOf(Input);
  // Assert
  Assert.AreEqual(Expected, Actual);
end;
```

---

[12]https://github.com/VSoftTechnologies/DUnitX

Write simple, "right down the middle" tests first

The first tests you write should be the simplest tests – the "happy path," They should be the ones that easily and basically illustrate the functionality you are trying to write. If you are writing an addition algorithm, the early tests that you write should make sure that your code can do 2 + 2 = 4. Then, once those tests pass, you should start writing the more complicated tests (as discussed below) that test the edges and boundaries of your code.

Write tests that test the edges

Once the basics are tested and you know that your basic functionality works, you should test "the edges." That is, you should test what happens if an overflow occurs. What if values go to zero or below zero? What if they go to `MaxInt`? `MinInt`? If you doing something with geometry, what if you try to create an arc of 361 degrees? What happens if you pass in an empty string? A string that is 2GB in size? A good set of tests will explore the outer edges of what might happen to a given method.

Test across boundaries

Unit tests should test both sides of a given boundary. If you are building some tests for `TDateTime`, try testing one second before midnight and one second after. Test across the date value of `0.0`. If you are dealing with a structure that holds a rectangle, then test what happens to points inside and outside the rectangle. What about above or below? To the left or right? Above and to the right? Below and to the left? Moving across boundaries are places where your code might fail or perform in unpredictable ways.

If you can, test the entire spectrum

If it is practical, test the entire set of possibilities for your functionality. If it involves an enumerated type, test the functionality with every one of the items in the enumeration. It might be impractical to test every possible string or every integer, but if you can test every possibility, do it.

If possible, cover every code path

This one is challenging as well, but if your code is designed for testing, and you make use of a code coverage tool, you can ensure that every line of your code is covered by unit tests at least once. Delphi has a very good code coverage tool available for your use[13]. Use it in concert with your unit tests. Covering every code path won't guarantee that there aren't any bugs, but it surely gives you valuable information about the state of every line of code.

---

[13]https://code.google.com/p/delphi-code-coverage/

Write tests that reveal a bug, then fix it

This is a powerful and useful technique. If you find a bug, write a test that reveals it. Then, you can easily fix the bug by debugging the test. Then you have a nice regression test to make sure that if that bug comes back for any reason, you'll know right away. It's really easy to fix a bug when you have a simple, straightforward test to run in the debugger.

A side benefit here is that you've "tested your test." Because you've seen the test fail and then have seen it pass, you know that the test is valid in that it has proven to work correctly. This makes it an even better regression test.

Make each test independent of each other

Tests should never depend on each other. If your tests have to be run in a certain order, then you need to change your tests. Instead, you should make proper use of the Setup and TearDown features of your unit testing framework to ensure each test is ready to run individually. Unit tests frameworks don't guarantee that tests are going to be run in any particular order, and if your tests depend on tests running in a specific order, then you may find yourself with some subtle, hard to track down bugs in your tests themselves. Make sure each test stands alone, and you won't have this problem.

Write one assert per test

You should write one assert per test. If you can't do that, then refactor your tests so that your SetUp and TearDown events are used to correctly create the environment so that each test can be run individually. If your tests require elaborate setup and you feel the need to run multiple tests and call `Check`/`Assert` multiple times, then you need to create a new test case class and utilize its `Setup`/`TearDown` feature for that particular test case, enabling you to create multiple tests for the specific situation.

Name your tests clearly. Don't be afraid of long names.

Since you are doing one assert per test, each test can end up being very specific. Thus, don't be afraid to use a long, complete test name. It is better to have `TestDivisionWhenNumPositiveDenomNegative` than `DivisionTest3`. A long complete name lets you know immediately what test failed and what exactly what the test was trying to do. Long, clearly named tests also can document your tests. For example, a test named "DivisionByZeroShouldThrowException" documents exactly what the code does when you try to divide by 0.

Test that every raised exception is in fact raised.

If your code raises exceptions, then write tests to ensure that every exception you raise in fact gets raised when it is supposed to. Both DUnit and DUnitX have the ability to test for an exception being raised, so you should use that feature to ensure that every exception your code raises is indeed raised under the proper circumstances.

Avoid the use of CheckTrue or Assert.IsTrue

Avoid checking for a Boolean condition. For instance, instead of checking if two things are equal with CheckTrue or Assert.IsTrue, use CheckEquals or Assert.AreEqual instead. Why? Because this:

```
CheckTrue(Expected, Actual)
```

will report something like "*Some test failed: Expected True but actual result was False*". That doesn't tell you anything. Instead, use CheckEquals:

```
CheckEquals(Expected, Actual)
```

which will tell you the actual values involved, such as "*Some test failed: Expected 7 but actual result was 3.*"

Constantly run your tests

Run your tests while you are writing code. Your tests should run fast, enabling you to run them after even minor changes. If you can't run your tests as part of your normal development process then something is going wrong – unit tests are supposed to run almost instantly. If they aren't, it's probably because you aren't running them in isolation.

Run your tests as part of every automated build.

Just as you should be running your tests as you develop, they should also be an integral part of your continuous integration process. A failed test should mean that your build is broken. Don't let a failing test linger – consider it a build failure and fix it immediately.

13.5 Test Driven Development

Probably the most controversial facet of unit testing is the question "When should I write my tests?" This question is controversial because the rise of unit testing coincided with the rise of the notion of Test Driven Development, or TDD. TDD says that you should write unit tests first, before anything else, and that your tests should drive your code and your design.

Some people object to TDD because they say that adding the writing of tests will add time to the project and make it either late or longer. Proponents say that the time spent up front will save more time in the long run because your code will work right the first time and you'll have a set of tests to prove it. I'm not here to settle this debate or even to engage much in it. Whether you decide to test first, test in the middle, or test after, I just want you to write tests.

The basic idea behind TDD is the notion of "Red, Green, Refactor." In other words, write tests that fail, write code that makes the tests pass, refactor your code so it is clean, and start again. The tests you write should define the correct behavior you want from your code. You then write code to make the tests pass. You then can improve – refactor – the code to improve it, all the while making sure your tests still pass. Once you are satisfied, you move on to the next requirement of your code, starting with a new test.

> The Red/Green part comes from unit testing tools that show failed tests in red and passing tests in green. Unit test proponents are happy when they "see green" in their testing tool.

You repeat this cycle until your code is complete and all requirements are met. At the end, you have code that can be proven, via your unit tests, to do what it was defined and required to do. The tests then also serve as a regression suite to ensure that any subsequent changes you make don't break the designed, required functionality.

That's a very quick overview of unit testing. For a more in depth view, I recommend the seminal work on the subject by Kent Beck called "Test Driven Development: By Example"[14]. In this book, Beck lays out the entire case for TDD and takes you through the entire process. It is a must read for anyone interested in unit testing and TDD.

Although it's a complete change of development mindset, when you use TDD, the tendency is to write decoupled code: you are writing the tests first, and then you must write the code. If you write coupled code, you cannot run the test; therefore, you will design it in a decoupled way so that it can be safely tested. Another great advantage lies in the Refactor phase - in that phase you will see new ways to write your code (and learn a lot). Usually in this phase you will see a lot of code smells[15] and rewrite your code to remove them. After some time, your code is more decoupled and clean.

13.6 A Basic Example

So far all we've had is a lot of theory, so how about a little practice?

Let's say we have a requirement to write a class that does basic mathematical actions. It needs to add, subtract, multiply, divide, and provide a Power function (that is, x raised to the y). For simplicity's sake, we'll assume all the math will be done with integers.

And here's what we are going to do:

1. Write a test
2. Write code until the application compiles but the test fails

---

[14]http://www.amazon.com/gp/product/0321146530/ref=as_li_ss_tl?ie=UTF8&camp=1789&creative=390957&creativeASIN=0321146530&linkCode=as2&tag=nickhodgeshomepa

[15]http://en.wikipedia.org/wiki/Code_smell

3. Write code until the test passes
4. Refactor until we are happy with our code
5. Go to step 1

And we'll do this until we are done and our class does everything it is supposed to do and we have tests that prove it.

So following TDD, the first thing we need to do is to write tests. We'll use the DUnitX testing suite because it is easier to use in our examples. Here's a class that will do a very basic test of our addition algorithm:

```
unit uCalculatorTests;

interface

uses
      uCalculator
    , DUnitX.TestFramework
    ;

type
  [TestFixture]
  TCalculatorTests = class
  private
    Expected, Actual: integer;
    Calculator: TCalculator;
    [Setup]
    procedure Setup;
    [TearDown]
    procedure TearDown;
  public
    [Test]
    procedure TestSimpleAddition;
  end;

implementation

procedure TCalculatorTests.Setup;
begin
  Calculator := TCalculator.Create;
end;

procedure TCalculatorTests.TearDown;
```

```
begin
   Calculator.Free;
end;


procedure TCalculatorTests.TestSimpleAddition;
begin
  Expected := 4;
  Actual := Calculator.Add(2, 2);
  Assert.AreEqual(Expected, Actual, 'The calculator thinks that 2 + 2 is not 4!');
end;


end.
```

This is our first exposure to DUnitX, so some discussion is in order. First, the uses clause includes DUnitX.TestFramework. That unit is all you should need to include when building tests. It includes all the classes and interfaces you need to declare and write unit tests using the framework.

Next, you can declare a class as a "test fixture" by tagging it with the [TestFixture] attribute. A Test Fixture is a class that contains tests. Any class will do – it doesn't matter what the class descends from, as long as it contains that attribute, it will be scanned for tests. This makes it pretty easy to write tests, as you don't have to descend from a particular class as you do in the DUnit framework.

In order to declare an actual test, you add a method to your Test Fixture that has the [Test] attribute attached to it. By convention, I like to make these methods public. Any method that has the [Test] attribute will be run by the DUnitX framework.

It is also common to declare a set of common fields in the private section of the Test Fixture. Very often, test methods will all require a similar set of variables, and it makes sense to declare them as class fields. In the above case, there are two variables, Expected and Actual, that will likely be used by every test, so they are declared in common.

We are going to be testing the TCalculator class, so naturally we'll need an instance of TCalculator. Each test should run completely independent of each other, and so we'll want to create a new instance for every test. We could do that in each [Test] method, but that would be tedious. Unit testing frameworks normally provide a means for simplifying this repetitive process via the notion of "Setup" and "TearDown." Via the aptly named attributes [Setup] and [TearDown], you can write code that will be called for every test. Thus, in our case, we can create and destroy an instance of TCalculator for each test. Any method tagged with the [Setup] attribute will be run at the start of every test, and any method tagged with the [TearDown] attribute will be run at the end of every test.

Though not shown here, you can also do Setup and TearDown at the Test Fixture level by declaring methods on the Test Fixture with the [SetUpFixture] and [TearDownFixture] attributes. Any methods declared with these attributes will be run at the creation and destruction of the Test Fixture, respectively. You should only have one of each of these attributes in your class.

In order for an actual test to be run, you must call a method of the `Assert` class. `Assert` has a number of class methods on it that do the actual testing. The `Assert` class is defined in the `DUnitX.TestFramework` unit. You can see it there. `Assert` allows you to check most anything and has many overloads to ensure that you can test any data type.

All of the methods take an optional final parameter of type `string`. This allows you to add your own message on to the call to `Assert` so that you can explain the exact nature of the error based on the test. You can use this string to uniquely identify the test error and completely explain why it failed. This makes finding and fixing failing tests much easier. Don't be afraid to provide a complete, specific message explaining the problem.

Okay, back to our example. Now here's the fun part: Our code won't compile. It claims to use a unit called `uCalculator`, but that unit is completely empty right now. We haven't written any code for it yet because we wrote our test first. And it's a really simple test – checking to see if our calculator can figure out that two and two is four. Not a tough test, but a critical one. If that doesn't work, then nothing will.

So, in our TDD example here, our first step is done: we've written a test. The second step: get the code to compile.

In order to do that, we'll create a `TCalculator` class with an `Add` method:

```
unit uCalculator;

interface

type
  TCalculator = class
    function Add(x, y: integer): integer;
  end;

implementation

{ TCalculator }

function TCalculator.Add(x, y: integer): integer;
begin

end;

end.
```

Okay, so now the code compiles. It doesn't do anything, and our test still fails, but it compiles. Step Two is complete.

For Step Three, we'll write code until our test passes. The first thing that we need to do is to register our test class. In order for DUnitX to do its magic, it needs to know that our Test Fixture is available for testing. Thus, in the initialization section of our test unit we'll add the following:

```
initialization
  TDUnitX.RegisterTestFixture(TCalculatorTests);
```

Next, we'll update our DPR file to actually run DUnitX code. First, we'll add these three units to the uses clause:

```
  DUnitX.TestFramework,
  DUnitX.Loggers.Console,
  DUnitX.Windows.Console,
```

DUnitX.TestFramework is the unit that contains all the code for DUnitX's main interface.

DUnitX.Loggers.Console contains a class that implements ILogger. The ILogger interface is the one that provides the output of the tests. In this case, the unit includes the TDUnitXConsoleLogger class that outputs the test results to the console.

DUnitX.Windows.Console contains a cool class that provide colors to the console, allowing us to do things like output green results for passing tests, red results for failing tests, and purple for setup code.

Then we have to declare three variables:

```
var
  Runner: ITestRunner;
  Logger: ITestLogger;
  Results: ITestResults;
```

Runner is the interface that will actually run the tests. Logger is the reference to the console runner discussed above. And Results is the interface that will hold the results of the tests. We won't actually do anything with the results in our simple example, but if you wanted to log or otherwise record the results somewhere, you could do this using the Results variable.

Then, we'll use those variables in the DPR file:

```
try
  //Create the runner
  Runner := TDUnitX.CreateRunner;
  Runner.UseRTTI := True;
  //tell the runner how we will log things
  Logger := TDUnitXConsoleLogger.Create;
  Runner.AddLogger(Logger);
  //Run tests
  Results := Runner.Execute;
  System.Write('Done.. press the <Enter> key to quit.');
  System.Readln;
except
  on E: Exception do
    System.Writeln(E.ClassName, ': ', E.Message);
end;
```

Basically we create and use the runner. This is fairly boilerplate code, so I won't discuss it too much. It just runs the tests, displays the output in the console, and waits for you to press the Enter key.

The real fun is that the code will now compile and run. Sure, the test fails, but we have more code to write. We'll keep writing until the test passes.

And making the test pass is really easy. How about this:

```
function TCalculator.Add(x, y: integer): integer;
begin
  Result := 4;
end;
```

Now, we run our test, and it passes. Yay!

At this point, let's add another test.

```
procedure TCalculatorTests.AddingOneAndOneShouldReturnTwo;
begin
  Expected := 2;
  Actual := Calculator.Add(1, 1);
  Assert.AreEqual(Expected, Actual, 'The calculator thinks that 1 + 1 is not 2!');
end;
```

Now we'll run both tests, and – uh-oh – that new test doesn't pass. Looks like it's time to refactor by changing the code in our Add function to fix it.

In order to make both of the tests pass, we need to actually do an addition algorithm. How about this one:

```
function TCalculator.Add(x, y: integer): integer;
begin
  Result := (x + 6 + y - y + y - 6) * 2 div 2;
end;
```

(I know, it's ridiculous, but it works. Bear with me....)

Yay! Now we have passing tests! Step Three complete!

So let's keep refactoring. Clearly the above algorithm will work just fine – it gets the correct result for addition. But I'm guessing that a better one exists.

How about this:

```
function TCalculator.Add(x, y: integer): integer;
begin
  Result := (x + y - y + y) * 2 div 2;
end;
```

If we change the algorithm to the above, our test still passes. We've made changes, and our tests still pass, so we know that our changes are safe. How about we add a test to test if we can properly add zero. That seems like a bit of an edge case:

```
procedure TCalculatorTests.TestAddingZero;
begin
  Expected := 4;
  Actual := Calculator.Add(4, 0);
  Assert.AreEqual(Expected, Actual, 'The calculator thinks that 4 + 0 is not 4!');
end;
```

Running that results in all of our tests passing.

How about adding negative numbers:

```
procedure TCalculatorTests.TestAddingTwoNegativeNumbers;
begin
  Expected := -4;
  Actual := Calculator.Add(-2, -2);
  Assert.AreEqual(Expected, Actual, 'The Add function failed to realize that -2 +\
  -2 is -4');
end;
```

That passes, as well. So now we can move on to Step Four with some confidence (I'll bet you can think of some other tests that might fit in here. What happens when you add a positive and a negative? What about sums that cross zero? Does all that work? I'll leave that as an exercise for the reader.).

Our addition algorithm is proving to be effective, but you aren't satisfied. It looks a little goofy, and you go to that Math PhD you know, and he suggests that you use the following instead:

```
function TCalculator.Add(x, y: integer): integer;
begin
  Result := x + y + 1;
end;
```

That looks a little simplistic, but a PhD is a PhD, and so you add the refactored test to your code. But uh oh! It fails all the tests. There must be a problem with the new algorithm. That's not good.

But what is good is that you know right away that there is an issue, and you have a set of tests that can be easily debugged to find the problem. No finding the bug after delivery to QA, no stepping through complex application code to find the issue – just a quick debugging session in a ready-made test to find the issue. In our case, that pesky "+ 1" is the issue. Remove that, and lo and behold, it works! All the tests pass! Step Four is now complete! WooHoo!

Step Five says to start the whole process over. In our case, we would a test for the Subtract method, see it fail, write code until it passes, refactor to our satisfaction, and then start in on Multiply and Divide. A simple example, yes, but it should give you a taste of what the process should be like and how you can use the simple five step pattern to write tests and code together.

And of course, the end result is a class that meets requirements and has a load of unit tests that can be used as regression tests and that give confidence that you can refactor and alter your code if desired without fear of things breaking. Your changes might break things, but you'll know immediately because you are running your tests constantly as you debug. Your tests can reveal bugs as you write them, and thus you can fix them immediately.

Now this example is a simple one. The tests all lack something that would probably be very prevalent in your real code – dependencies. As previously noted above, the key thing that you need to do when unit testing is test classes *in isolation*, meaning that the tests for the class should not be dependent on anything. As discussed above, dependencies need to be faked, and so in the next chapter, we'll look at how you can create fake classes to take the place of real dependencies in order to properly isolate your classes for proper testing.

14 Testing with an Isolation Framework

In the previous chapter, we looked at the whys and hows of unit testing. We went through a very simple example of how to do Test Driven Development. But as I mentioned at the close of the chapter, it was simple – too simple, in fact for real world use.

In previous chapters, I have stressed many things, but particularly the notion of testing your code in isolation, and the decoupling of your code via Dependency Injection. So now, it's time for it all to come together. The proper use of Dependency Injection should make testing your classes in isolation a piece of cake. I exhorted you to create a testing executable that could run on any machine without any specific dependencies present. But if you are going to do that, you'll have to substitute your actual dependencies with ones that don't actually couple to anything "real". If only there were a way to do that simply and easily.

Hah – by now you should know that I drop the "If only" on you, there will be a way to do that: in this case, it's Isolation Frameworks. We discussed them a bit in the last chapter, talking about the difference between Stubs and Mocks and how you can use them to test your classes in isolation. I promised that in this chapter we'd dive deeper into unit testing by showing how to use fakes – that is, stubs and mocks – to be able to test almost any code with any dependencies.

14.1 A Quick Review

Okay, first, let's do a quick review. First, an isolation framework is a set of classes that enables you to provide fake dependencies for your classes. There are two kinds of fakes – stubs and mocks. Stubs do nothing other than the very minimum to replace their real counterpart. A test success or failure won't depend on a stub, and generally, a stub will do nothing. A test should never fail because of a stub. A mock, however, is a fake representation that can and should provide feedback and information to a given test. In fact, the reason to use a mock instead of a stub is to interact with the Class Under Test and provide the ability to fail the test. That is the big distinction between a mock and a stub: a mock can fail a test where a stub never should.

14.2 Isolation Frameworks for Delphi

While there were mocking frameworks for Delphi before the introduction of virtual interfaces and generics, a true and complete isolation framework really wasn't available until XE2. The Delphi

Mocks Framework[1] (as noted, it is common to call Isolation Frameworks "Mock Frameworks") is an open source project built by none other than Vincent Parrett of FinalBuilder[2] fame – yes, the same guy that leads the development of the DUnitX project (He's a busy guy....). You can download and install Delphi Mocks using Git (See the Resources section at the end of the book for resources to help you learn Git.).

14.3 Getting Started

In their simplest form, a fake object is an alternate implementation of a class that provides "fake" responses to method calls. For example, you have an interface ICustomer that has a method GetCustomerName, and normally, that call goes to the production database and gets the name (a simple, unlikely example, I know, but you get the idea). So to avoid the call to the database, you just create MockCustomer and implement its call to GetCustomerName and have it return "George Jetson" every time. This enables you to test the class that is using ICustomer without having to hit the database at all.

But that can get a bit clumsy. What if you want to return different values based on different inputs? What if you find a bug based on specific input or output, and you want to create a unit test for that specific case? What if you don't want to return anything at all because you are testing something different, but need to call to GetCustomerName? Then a specially created fake class as described above gets harried, complicated, and hard to maintain.

Enter an Isolation Framework

What if we could have a framework that would allow us to implement any interface and define easily and exactly what the inputs and outputs should be? That would be cool. This would enable you to easily create a fake object that can respond to method calls in defined ways in a flexible, easy to set up manner. This is what an isolation framework does.

Obviously something this flexible needs some powerful language features. Such a framework would have to be able to flex to dynamically implement an interface. It would have to be able to dynamically recognize method calls and respond accordingly. Fortunately, as of XE2, Delphi is up to the task. As we saw in a previous chapter, Delphi XE2 introduced the TVirtualInterface class that lets you dynamically implement any interface at run-time. Combine that with the new RTTI, and you have the ability to build a very powerful mocking framework.

A Simple Stub

The Delphi Mocks Framework can easily create a simple stub for you to use to stub out a dependency that you don't need for a given test. For instance, say you had a class as follows:

---

[1]https://github.com/VSoftTechnologies/Delphi-Mocks
[2]https://github.com/VSoftTechnologies/Delphi-Mocks

```
type
  TDollarToGalleonsConverter = class
  private
    FLogger: ILogger;
  public
    constructor Create(aLogger: ILogger);
    function ConvertDollarsToGalleons(aDollars: Double; aExchangeRate: Double):\
Double;
  end;
```

```
    function TDollarToGalleonsConverter.ConvertDollarsToGalleons(aDollars, aExcha\
ngeRate: Double): Double;
    begin
      Result := aDollars * aExchangeRate;
      FLogger.Log(Format('Converted %f dollars to %f Galleons', [aDollars, Result\
]));
    end;
```

```
    constructor TDollarToGalleonsConverter.Create(aLogger: ILogger);
    begin
      inherited Create;
      FLogger := aLogger;
    end;
```

It has a single dependency of type ILogger, which passed to it via constructor injection. Normally, the logger will make an entry in the database every time you convert Dollars to Galleons, but you don't want that to happen for fake transactions that will happen when you run your unit tests. Instead, you'd like to simply ignore the logging as part of testing of the conversion. In other words, you want a stub for the ILogger interfaces.

First, let's look at ILogger:

```
type
  ILogger = interface(IInvokable)
  ['{B571A28D-A576-4C83-A0D3-CB211435CDEA}']
    procedure Log(aString: string);
  end;
```

This is a typical interface with one exception – it augments the IInvokable interface. IInvokable is simply an interface that has the {M+} switch turned on. This is required by the Delphi Mocks Framework in order for it to stub or mock and interface. It is probably a good idea to descend all of your interfaces from IInvokable for this reason.

Once you have your class ready to test, here's a test that you can write that creates a stub for ILogger and lets you focus on testing the conversion process:

```
procedure TDollarToGalleonConverterTest.TestPointFiveCutsDollarsinHalf;
var
  Expected: Double;
  Actual: Double;
  TempConverter: TDollarToGalleonsConverter;
  TempLogger: TMock<ILogger>;
begin
  //Arrange
  TempLogger := TMock<ILogger>.Create;
  TempConverter := TDollarToGalleonsConverter.Create(TempLogger);
  try
    Expected := 1.0;
    //Act
    Actual := TempConverter.ConvertDollarsToGalleons(2, 0.5);
    //Assert
    Assert.AreEqual(Expected, Actual, 'Converter failed to convert 2 dollars to 1\
galleon');
  finally
    TempConverter.Free;
  end;
end;
```

Creating the stub is as simple as creating an instance of TMock<ILogger>. TMock is a generic record that takes an interface. The interface has to have the {M+} compiler flag attached to it. You can either add the directive yourself or descend all your interfaces from IInvokable as mentioned above. Once a TMock<T> is created, it assumes the role of the interface type passed to it. Thus, you can pass the resulting type to the constructor of TDollarToGalleonConverter class and none shall be the wiser. If the class calls methods on the logger, they will be ignored by the fake instances of ILogger.

Thus, that is all there is to creating a simple stub interface for use in our tests. You can now test TDollarToGalleanCoverter.ConvertDollarsToGalleons in isolation, apart from any specific implementation of a logger.

Testing the Logger

Now you've written tests to ensure that the currency converter works as it should. But you still have something else to test – that is, does the logger actually do what it is supposed to do when you make a conversion? You expect (remember that word) that the logger will make a single call to the Log method whenever a conversion occurs, but how can you check to make sure that actually happens and that the class using the Logger is using it correctly?

This is where the second kind of fake comes in – mocks. We discussed before that Mocks are a fake class that actively takes part in a unit test and can actually fail a test. In our case we want a mock that will make sure that the Log method will be called and that the correct thing will be logged.

Consider the following test:

```
procedure TDollarToGalleonConverterTest.TestThatLoggerIsProperlyCalled;
var
  Expected: Double;
  Actual: Double;
  TempConverter: TDollarToGalleonsConverter;
  TempLogger: TMock<ILogger>;
  Input: Double;
  TempMessage: string;
begin
  //Arrange
  TempLogger := TMock<ILogger>.Create;
  Input := 2.0;
  Expected := 1.0;
  TempMessage := Format('Converted %f dollars to %f Galleons', [Input, Expect\
ed]);
  TempLogger.Setup.Expect.Once.When.Log(TempMessage);
  TempConverter := TDollarToGalleonsConverter.Create(TempLogger);
  try
    //Act
    Actual := TempConverter.ConvertDollarsToGalleons(Input, 0.5);
    //Assert
    TempLogger.Verify();
  finally
    TempConverter.Free;
  end;

end;
```

Some things to note:

- The setup for the mock must be done before the mock is sent to the Class Under Test.
- The setup code for the mock is using a fluent interface, where each call leads to the next. One could read the code as *"For the TempLogger, do the setup by expecting that the method will be called once, and when it is, it will be passed a given string"*
- The call to Verify is the assertion that you are making for the test. This is how a mock can fail the test. If the things that were expected didn't happen, Verify will raise an exception and fail the test.

- You can set up as many expectations for a given mock as you want. You can expect that things will happen Once, Never, AtLeastOnce, Exactly a specified number of times, AtLeast a number of times, AtMost a number of times, Between a number of times, or Before and After other methods. In each case, you can also specify exactly what parameters are passed When that specific call is made.

- In other words, you can Expect whatever you want to have happen to the class during the test, and if those specified things don't happen in the way you say that they should happen, then the test will fail.

- The When property returns an instance of the interface itself, so that is the point where you will make the call to the method of the interface you want to test. There you pass all the parameters as they would be passed in the test itself.

Stubs That Do Stuff

Sometimes in the process of testing you need your stub to return a value from a function call. As your tests run, you know that your CUT will be calling a function on your stub, and you want it to behave in a predetermined way. No problem – Delphi Mocks allows you to tell your stubs to return values of functions. Instead of calling Expect, you can call WillReturn, passing to it an expected value as well as the actual method call with parameters via the When method.

Consider the following interface and implementing class:

```delphi
unit uCreditCardValidator;

interface

uses
    SysUtils;

type
  ICreditCardValidator = interface(IInvokable)
  ['{68553321-248C-4FD4-9881-C6B6B92B95AD}']
    function IsCreditCardValid(aCreditCardNumber: string): Boolean;
    procedure DoNotCallThisEver;
  end;

  TCreditCardValidator = class(TInterfacedObject, ICreditCardValidator)
    function IsCreditCardValid(aCreditCardNumber: string): Boolean;
    procedure DoNotCallThisEver;
  end;

  ECreditCardValidatorException = class(Exception);
```

```
implementation

uses
    Dialogs;

function TCreditCardValidator.IsCreditCardValid(aCreditCardNumber: string): Boole\
an;
begin
  // Let's pretend this calls a SOAP server that charges $0.25 everytime
  // you use it.

  // For Demo purposes, we'll have the card be invalid if it the number 7 in it
  Result := Pos('7', aCreditCardNumber) <= 0;
  WriteLn('Ka-Ching! You were just charged $0.25');
  if not Result then
  begin
    raise ECreditCardValidatorException.Create('Bad Credit Card!  Do not accept!'\
);
  end;
end;


procedure TCreditCardValidator.DoNotCallThisEver;
begin
  // This one will charge the company $500!  We should never
  // call this!
end;


end.
```

This code (pretends) to validate credit cards. It "charges" your company $0.25 every time you use it, so it is a dependency that performs an action that you need in order to test the class that uses it, but one that you obviously don't want to have run every time your tests run.

Here's a class that uses it:

```
unit uCreditCardManager;

interface

uses
      uCreditCardValidator
    , SysUtils
    ;

type
  TCreditCardManager = class
  private
    FCCValidator: ICreditCardValidator;
  public
    constructor Create(aCCValidator: ICreditCardValidator);
    function CreditCardIsValid(aCCString: string): Boolean;
    function ProcessCreditCard(aCCString: string; aAmount: Double): Double;
  end;


  EBadCreditCard = class(Exception);

implementation

function TCreditCardManager.CreditCardIsValid(aCCString: string): Boolean;
begin
  inherited;
  Result := FCCValidator.IsCreditCardValid(aCCString);
end;

function TCreditCardManager.ProcessCreditCard(aCCString: string; aAmount: Double)\
: Double;
begin
  if CreditCardIsValid(aCCString) then
  begin
    // Charge the card
    Result := aAmount;
  end else
  begin
    Result := 0.0;
  end;
end;
```

```
constructor TCreditCardManager.Create(aCCValidator: ICreditCardValidator);
begin
  inherited Create;
  FCCValidator := aCCValidator;
end;


end.
```

The TCreditCardManager class has a dependency on ICreditCardValidator. But if you want to test TCreditCardManager, you don't want to depend on the real implementation of ICreditCardValidator because that wouldn't allow your tests to run in isolation. However, when you test TCreditCardManager, you need the ICreditCardValidator to behave in a certain way – either accept or reject the card. You can tell the stub exactly what to do.

Here's the test for a passing card:

```
procedure TestTCCValidator.TestCardChargeReturnsProperAmountWhenCardIsGood;
var
  CCManager: TCreditCardManager;
  CCValidator: TMock<ICreditCardValidator>;
  GoodCard: String;
  Input: Double;
  Expected, Actual: Double;
begin
  //Arrange
  GoodCard := '123456';
  Input := 49.95;
  Expected := Input;
  CCValidator := TMock<ICreditCardValidator>.Create;
  CCValidator.Setup.WillReturn(True).When.IsCreditCardValid(GoodCard);

  CCManager := TCreditCardManager.Create(CCValidator);
  try
    //Act
    Actual := CCManager.ProcessCreditCard(GoodCard, Input)
  finally
    CCManager.Free;
  end;
  // Assert
  Assert.AreEqual(Expected, Actual);
end;
```

Here, we call WillReturn(True) on the stub, allowing the credit card manager to return the proper amount charged. Next, we can tell the stub to return False for the validation and make sure that the credit card manager returns zero in that case. The stub then doesn't affect whether the test passes or fails, it merely exists purely for the purpose of letting the actual test run in the way that you want it to run.

Here is the test to ensure that the credit card manager returns $0.00 when the card is invalid:

```
procedure TestTCCValidator.TestCardChargeReturnsZeroWhenCCIsBad;
var
  CCManager: TCreditCardManager;
  CCValidator: TMock<ICreditCardValidator>;
  GoodCard: String;
  Input: Double;
  Expected, Actual: Double;
begin
  //Arrange
  GoodCard := '777777';  // 7 in a card makes it bad.....
  Input := 49.95;
  Expected := 0;
  CCValidator := TMock<ICreditCardValidator>.Create;
  // Tell the stub to make it a bad card
  CCValidator.Setup.WillReturn(False).When.IsCreditCardValid(GoodCard);

  CCManager := TCreditCardManager.Create(CCValidator);
  try
    //Act
    Actual := CCManager.ProcessCreditCard(GoodCard, Input)
  finally
    CCManager.Free;
  end;
  // Assert
  Assert.AreEqual(Expected, Actual);
end;
```

Dependencies that Do Expected Things

Stubs are fakes that do nothing, or at least don't do anything that can cause the test to fail. In fact, a Stub might be defined as a fake for which you have no declared expectations. Mocks, on the other hand, are fakes that do cause tests to fail and which do have declared expectations. Often the reason for that failure is that your class under test interacts with a dependency in an unexpected way.

Mocks allow you to ensure that the interactions with a dependency are what is expected. TMock<T> allows you to state what the expectations are for a given interaction with a dependency and then to verify that those expectations were met.

For instance, here is a simple class that manages a mailing list. It can take names and email addresses, and send out single or bulk emails (Okay, it can't do anything at all like that – it only pretends to do that. But this is a simple demo.). Anyway, here's the class:

```
TEmailListManager = class
private
  FEmailSender: IEmailSender;
public
  constructor Create(aEmailSender: IEmailSender);
  procedure RegisterNewPerson(aName: string; aEmailAddress: string);
end;


...


constructor TEmailListManager.Create(aEmailSender: IEmailSender);
begin
  inherited Create;
  FEmailSender := aEmailSender;
end;


procedure TEmailListManager.RegisterNewPerson(aName, aEmailAddress: string);
begin
  // Insert person and email address into database
  // Then send a confirmation email
  FEmailSender.SendMail(aEmailAddress, 'Thanks for signing up'!);
end;
```

This class merely pretends to keep track of people who sign up for a mailing list. The important thing here is the code in the RegisterNewPerson method, where it uses its dependency to send a single email confirming that a person has signed up.

If you want to test this class, you don't actually want it to send out emails – you want to fake that part. But when you test adding someone to the database (note that I have for simplicity's sake left out the dependency which would do that), you want to be sure that the dependency actually does make a call to the code that would send out that email. This is, again, what Mocks do – they validate that sort of thing.

So in order to do that, you'd write the following test:

```
procedure TEmailManagerTester.TestAddingPersonSendingOneEmail;
var
  CUT: TEmailListManager;
  MockSender: TMock<IEmailSender>;
  StubSL: TMock<TStringList>;
begin
  // Arrange

  MockSender := TMock<IEmailSender>.Create;
  MockSender.Setup.Expect.Once.When.SendMail(TestEmail, TestMessage);
  MockSender.Setup.Expect.Never.When.SendBulkEmail;

  CUT := TEmailListManager.Create(MockSender);
  try
    // Act
    CUT.RegisterNewPerson('Marvin Martian', TestEmail);
  finally
    CUT.Free;
  end;

  // Assert
  MockSender.Verify();

end;
```

Here are some things to note:

- A mock can set up any number of expectations for a given test. In this case, MockSender creates two expectations that need to be met for the test to pass.
- First, it expects that the SendMail procedure will be called Once and only once. If it is called more than once or not at all, the test will fail.
- Second, it ensures that the SendBulkEmail method is Never called during the process of signing someone up. If it is called, then the test will fail.
- In order to determine whether or not the test passes, a call is made to MockSender.Verify. If the expectations are met, then the call does nothing. If an expectation is not met, then the call will raise an exception, resulting in a failing test.

In this way, you can make sure that your Class Under Test is doing the proper things with your dependencies without actually having to create a real dependency.

Dependencies That Raise Exceptions

Often, your dependencies will raise exceptions, and you need to ensure that your testing class handles that properly. Here's an interface and an implementing class that raises an exception when you try to validate a bad widget. In this case, we need a Mock, because we want to let the test pass or fail depending on whether or not the dependency raises the exception as expected. Basically, any time you are using a fake and you can call the Verify method, you are using a mock.

So for example, consider this unit:

```
unit uDependencyRaisesObjection;

interface

uses
    SysUtils
  ;

type
  IWidget = interface(IInvokable)
    function IsValid: Boolean;
  end;

  TWidget = class(TInterfacedObject, IWidget)
  public
    function IsValid: Boolean;
  end;

  IWidgetProcessor = interface(IInvokable)
    procedure ProcessWidget(aWidget: IWidget);
  end;

  TWidgetProcessor = class(TInterfacedObject, IWidgetProcessor)
  public
    procedure ProcessWidget(aWidget: IWidget);
  end;

  EInvalidWidgetException = class(Exception);

implementation

procedure TWidgetProcessor.ProcessWidget(aWidget: IWidget);
begin
```

```pascal
  try
    if aWidget.IsValid then
    begin
      WriteLn('Widget has been properly processed');
    end;
  except
    On E: EInvalidWidgetException do
    begin
      WriteLn('IsValid failed to validate the widget');
    end;
  end;
end;


function TWidget.IsValid: Boolean;
begin
  // Just for demo purposes, lets say that 1 in 100 widgets are bad
  // But then again, we'll never call this code because it will be mocked out
  Result := Random(100) >= 99;
  if not Result then
  begin
    raise EInvalidWidgetException.Create('Bad Widget! Bad, bad widget!');
  end;
end;


end.
```

In it you should notice that the `TWidget.IsValid` call has the potential to raise an exception. The `TWidgetProcessor` class uses `TWidget`, and thus should know what to do in the case of `TWidget` raising an `EInvalidWidgetException` exception. The `TWidgetProcessor.ProcessWidget` method has logic to properly handle the exception, but we want to test that, right?

In order to do that, we need to create a mock dependency based on `IWidget` that will raise the exception and make sure that `TWidgetProcessor` correctly handles it.

```pascal
procedure TTestWidgetProcessor.TestBadWidgetRaisedException;
var
  CUT: IWidgetProcessor;
  MockWidget: TMock<IWidget>;
begin
  // Arrange
  MockWidget := TMock<IWidget>.Create;
  MockWidget.Setup.WillRaise(EInvalidWidgetException).When.IsValid;
  CUT := TWidgetProcessor.Create;
```

```
  // Act
  CUT.ProcessWidget(MockWidget);
  // Assert
  MockWidget.Verify();
end;
```

This test is similar to the one in the previous section, except it establishes that a given exception type – EInvalidWidgetException – will be raised when IsValid is called. The test also makes sure that IsValid is only called once – no sense in letting code be called more than it need be.

Now you might look at that code above and say "But wait, you called IsValid, and yet it wasn't valid.". Well, yes – but remember, sometimes IsValid can raise an exception, and that is what you are telling the mock to do. In essence, the above code says "Call IsInvalid, raise an exception, and see if TWidgetProcessor handles the exception correctly. If it does, pass the test. If it doesn't, fail the test." Again, this is an example of a Mock determining whether or not a test fails.

Only One Mock Per Test

A given test should only ever have one mock per test. For instance, if you have a class that has three dependencies, you should always test that class with zero or one mocks and three or two stubs. You should never have two mocks because then you'd have two different ways for the tests to fail. Having only one mock means that the test can only fail one way. No matter how many dependencies you have, only one of them should be a Mock, and the rest should be stubs

Expectation Parameters Must Match

When you set an expectation and make a call to the interface, you must pass in parameters. Those parameters must then be used exactly as "expected" because if they are not, the Mock won't properly verify. In other words, those parameter values are expected just as much as the behavior itself. So for instance, if you set the following expectation

```
SomeMock.Setup.Expect.Once.When.Add(5, 9);
```

then that expectation will not be met if you call the actual test with

```
MyAdder.Add(4, 3);
```

The parameters must match exactly. If the parameter is a reference type, the reference must be exactly the same one – a different reference will cause the mock not to verify.

14.4 Conclusion

That should give you a good overview of Isolation Frameworks. Isolation Frameworks exist to allow you to test your classes in isolation. If you've used proper Dependency Injection, then testing your classes in isolation along with an Isolation Framework should be very easy. Stubs allow you to test classes by providing expectation-less fake classes and interfaces. Mocks allow you to test your class's interaction with its dependencies by providing numerous ways to verify that your Class Under Test behaved as expected when tested – all without having to create real dependencies.

Appendix A: Resources

Dependency Injection

- The best book on Dependency Injection is Dependency Injection in .Net by Mark Seamann[3]. The examples are all in C#, but don't be put off by that – it's an excellent, in-depth resource on a topic that I was only able to cover briefly.
- Mark's website[4] is also a great source of Dependency Injection information, Unit Testing, and general, all around techniques for writing good code.

Unit Testing

- The book I recommend on unit testing is "The Art of Unit Testing: With Examples in .NET"[5] by Roy Osherove. Again, the examples are in C#, but that's of little matter. What is important is the thorough, clear descriptions that Roy gives of all aspects of unit testing.
- The seminal book for Test Driven Development is entitled – surprise! – "Test Driven Development: By Example"[6] by Kent Beck. He pretty much originated the idea and the term.
- Another book to consider is the reference book entitled "xUnit Test Patterns."[7] This is a deep and thorough book on the topic of testing patterns. Seriously, it's a big, deep book. Really cool, though.
- Misko Hevery is a Google employee who writes extensively about writing testable code. You can read his blog[8] as well as watch the three videos below to see what Misko has to say on the subject of testing and testable code.
- The Clean Code Talks: Don't Look for Things[9]
- How to Write Clean, Testable Code[10]
- The Clean Code Talks – Unit Testing[11]

---

[3]http://www.amazon.com/gp/product/1935182501/ref=as_li_ss_tl?ie=UTF8&camp=1789&creative=390957&creativeASIN= 1935182501&linkCode=as2&tag=nickhodgeshomepa

[4]http://blog.ploeh.dk/

[5]http://www.amazon.com/gp/product/1617290890/ref=as_li_ss_tl?ie=UTF8&camp=1789&creative=390957&creativeASIN= 1617290890&linkCode=as2&tag=nickhodgeshomepa

[6]http://www.amazon.com/gp/product/0321146530/ref=as_li_ss_tl?ie=UTF8&camp=1789&creative=390957&creativeASIN= 0321146530&linkCode=as2&tag=nickhodgeshomepa

[7]http://www.amazon.com/gp/product/0131495054/ref=as_li_ss_tl?ie=UTF8&camp=1789&creative=390957&creativeASIN= 0131495054&linkCode=as2&tag=nickhodgeshomepa

[8]http://misko.hevery.com/

[9]http://www.youtube.com/watch?v=RlfLCWKxHJ0

[10]http://www.youtube.com/watch?v=XcT4yYu_TTs

[11]http://www.youtube.com/watch?v=wEhu57pih5w

Source Control

Most of the frameworks I recommend in the book are obtained via public source control repositories. Here are some links to get you started if you aren't familiar with Git, Mercurial, or Subversion.

Subversion

Git

- A nice, step-by-step tutorial that teaches Git Basics: http://gitimmersion.com/[12]
- An excellent, online book teaching Git: http://git-scm.com/book/en/[13]

Mercurial

- A simple and well-done tutorial for Mercurial is hginit.com[14]. It's specifically designed for people moving to a distributed source control system from a server-based world.
- The Mercurial team has a nice tutorial: http://mercurial.selenic.com/wiki/Tutorial[15]

Projects

- The Delphi Spring Framework: https://code.google.com/p/delphi-spring-framework/[16]
- The DUnitX Framework: https://github.com/VSoftTechnologies/DUnitX[17]
- The Delphi Sorcery Framework: https://code.google.com/p/delphisorcery/[18]
- The Delphi Mocks Framework: https://github.com/VSoftTechnologies/Delphi-Mocks[19]
- The OmniThread Library: https://code.google.com/p/omnithreadlibrary/[20]

General Good Stuff

- Mason Wheeler has an excellent discussion on Contravariance and Covariance: http://tech.turbu-rpg.com/149/generics-and-the-covariance-problem [21]
- Barry Kelly on closures and anonymous methods: http://blog.barrkel.com/2008/07/anonymous-method-details.html[22]

---

[12]http://gitimmersion.com/

[13]http://git-scm.com/book/en/

[14]http://hginit.com

[15]http://mercurial.selenic.com/wiki/Tutorial

[16]https://code.google.com/p/delphi-spring-framework/

[17]https://github.com/VSoftTechnologies/DUnitX

[18]https://code.google.com/p/delphisorcery/

[19]https://github.com/VSoftTechnologies/Delphi-Mocks

[20]https://code.google.com/p/omnithreadlibrary/

[21]http://tech.turbu-rpg.com/149/generics-and-the-covariance-problem

[22]http://blog.barrkel.com/2008/07/anonymous-method-details.html

Appendix B: My Delphi Story

In 1991, I was a newly-married, Lieutenant (jg) in the United States Navy. I had just come off of an overseas tour of ship duty. Life had slowed down considerably for me in my new job, and I was looking for a hobby. A friend of mine was talking about how he had written a flight and training scheduling application when he was in flight training, and that he'd used Turbo Pascal to do it. I was intrigued.

In the early 70's I had been taught BASIC in my Seventh Grade math class. You know:

```
200 REM *** MAKE A RANDOM LIST A(1) TO A(N)
210 A(1)=INT((N-1)*RND(1)+2)
220 FOR K=2 TO N
230 A(K)=INT(N*RND(1)+1)
240 FOR J=1 TO K-1
250 IF A(K)=A(J) THEN 230
260 NEXT J:NEXT K
```

etc. It was fun, and a couple of my friends and I actually built crude adventure games using it: "You are walking down the street and a bum asks you for a quarter: Do you....." We typed the programs in on punch hole tape, and ran it through on a teletype that was hooked to a computer at the University of Minnesota via one of those modems where you press the phone into the rubber cups. Wild to think about now.

I kept programming after school and ended up being a "Computer Rat" in tenth grade – the guy that would take everyone's punch cards and run them through the reader and then return them with the printout results. About that same time I finally discovered these strange things called "girls" and soon realized that these creatures didn't think much of computer rats, so my early programming career ended. Alas – had I stuck with it I might have ended up rich in Silicon Valley – my timing would have been perfect. But it was not to be.

When that Navy friend handed me a copy of Tom Swan's Programming Turbo Pascal 5.5 and a – ahem – copy of Turbo Pascal 5.5 on a floppy, I dove in with abandon. Hey, I was already married, so it was a perfect way to expand the brain and build something. It took me a while to understand how you could program without line numbers, but I got the hang of it. My first purchase was Turbo Pascal for (the then brand new) Windows 1.0. I soon upgraded to Turbo Pascal for Windows 1.5 with (gasp) syntax highlighting!

This was the heyday of the PC age – you could use your modem to download shareware from a local bulletin board! Windows 3.0 was just taking off and I was totally into it. I was downloading Windows shareware and trying it out by the bucket load. I was teaching myself Windows programming with

TPW and a book by Tom Swan called "Programming Turbo Pascal for Windows 3.0." (I still have this wonderful, and now very tattered, book). I wrote a piece of shareware called Sysback, which backed up all your important configuration files (all your INI files, AUTOEXEC.BAT, CONFIG.SYS, etc.). I sold it for $2, and I bet I sold a couple thousand copies – people actually sent me money through the mail. Looking back, I should have charged $10, but I didn't know about basic economics and didn't believe that some knucklehead Navy Lieutenant could produce something of value. ;-)

I had a million questions, and I was dedicated enough to participate on the CompuServe forums for Turbo Pascal using an offline reader called TapCIS. It was perfect for me because I was a long distance call away from the nearest Compuserve node, and it would get on, download and upload what I wanted, and get off, storing everything for off-line reading. This was actually back in the day when you had to pay by the minute for long-distance, plus the per-minute charges on Compuserve. The costs added up, but I was determined to learn and loved every minute of it. I didn't understand the difference between a PChar and a string or an OWL object and a Win32 API, but hey, I did manage to get my software to work, and I even made a little money.

Compuserve was enormously helpful, and I soon made friends with Borlanders such as Xavier Pacheco and Steve Teixeira. There was also a very dedicated group of volunteers called TeamB. I met such folks as Pat Ritchey, Kurt Barthelmess, and Steve Schafer. These guys all soon became my heroes, as I had quickly become a Borland Fan Boy. To be as smart and capable as a TeamB member was a dream.

In 1993, a very fortuitous thing happened – I was transferred to the Naval Post-graduate School in Monterey, CA to study Information Technology Management. This was only about an hour away from the new Borland campus, and I was able to attend the annual TeamB/Online picnic held in Scotts Valley every year. It was there that I finally got to meet my TeamB heroes and a bunch of other folks that worked at Borland. One of the guys I met at that first picnic was Zack Urlocker, then the Delphi Product Manager. I told Zack about my studies in Software Engineering, and he did something that I had only dreamed about – he signed me up for the Delphi field test. In the summer of 1994, Delphi was a code name for the next version of Turbo Pascal, and rumored to be a "VB Killer."

Joining the Delphi Field Test was truly a life-changing experience for me. I was able to get an early start on a truly ground-breaking technology. To me, the coolest thing about Delphi was the ease with which you could write native components in Delphi itself (Remember, this was a time when writing components meant creating VBX controls for use in Visual Basic with C++.). In time, TSmiley was born, and the Borland guys picked up on it and demoed it all over the world. I was a bit surprised and honored. During the beta I also added a WAV file player to my shareware repertoire. Using Delphi made it so easy, it was almost criminal.

The highlight of early 1995 was skipping school to attend the Software Development '95 conference. For the first time ever, Delphi was going to be shown publicly, and it was a sensation. The Borland booth was overwhelmed with people, the hourly demos were packed, and the whole place was abuzz with news of Delphi. The second morning Borland gave out a limited number of preview disks, and there was a near riot as people lined up to get one. That evening, Anders Hjelsberg demonstrated Delphi to a standing room only crowd, wowing them with the exception handling, the blazingly fast native compiler, and the amazingly powerful and easy to use VCL. It was truly a defining moment in the history of software development.

I was a dedicated and enthusiastic field tester. I started out asking a million questions, but by the end of the field test, I was answering as many questions as I was asking. Borland knew that Delphi was going to explode, and they looked to expand the size of TeamB. Imagine how I felt when at the TeamB picnic that summer they pulled me aside and asked if I'd be willing to join. It took about 0.0001 seconds for me to say yes, though I remember being very nervous and feeling inadequate.

However, it all worked out. I learned and learned, and eventually, in 2000, I got out of the Navy and started my new job working for Xapware, Xavier Pacheco's company. A year later I started my own company in the Twin Cities area of Minnesota and soon joined forces with two other developers to form Lemanix. For five years we provided Delphi consulting and training. It was great to be doing Delphi full time.

Then, in 2006, Borland made a fateful decision to divest themselves of their developer tools. Realizing that they needed to beef up the product in order to sell it, they decided it was time for a proper Product Manager. Allen Bauer called me and asked me if I would be interested. Replying only a little slower than I had to the TeamB invitation, I soon moved to Scotts Valley to take my dream job. Two years later, I switched jobs to be the R&D Manager. After two years of that, well, there was a "difference of opinion" and I was asked to leave. I then moved to Pennsylvania where I continued to work as a development manager in a Delphi shop. Currently, I'm a full time Delphi developer and Development Manager at Veeva Systems.

It has been a long run. It's been a great run. And the fun part is that it feels like it is all beginning again as Delphi makes the move to Mobile while still providing all the powerful, cool features that developers want. Things like Dependency Injection, Delphi Spring Framework, DSharp, and other cool tools all are making this a great time to be a Delphi developer.

Made in the USA
Las Vegas, NV
13 May 2024

89887313R00133